AF688031

Don’t Grow—Mutate

Don't Grow—Mutate

Matthew Petchinsky

1

Don't Grow—Mutate

By: Matthew Petchinsky

Disclaimer

Don't Grow—Mutate is a work of creative self-exploration, metaphor-driven insight, and personal empowerment. It is not a substitute for professional medical care, psychological treatment, legal counsel, financial advice, or any other licensed professional service. The material contained within this book is intended for educational, inspirational, and reflective purposes only.

This book uses the concept of *mutation* as a symbolic framework. Mutation, as referenced throughout the text, is not presented as a biological or medical process, nor as a recommendation to alter the body, mind, or behavior through unsafe or unverified means. Instead, mutation is used metaphorically to describe internal change—shifts in perception, identity, resilience, adaptation, and self-concept—particularly in response to adversity, trauma, limitation, or systemic pressure.

Readers should not interpret any content in this book as medical advice, mental health treatment, or a diagnostic tool. If you are experiencing physical illness, neurological symptoms, psychological distress, emotional crisis, or thoughts of self-harm, you are strongly encouraged to seek assistance from a qualified healthcare professional, licensed therapist, or emergency service provider.

This book may explore themes related to struggle, stagnation, disability, pain, failure, transformation, and social alienation. These themes are addressed through narrative, symbolism, and personal insight rather than clinical instruction. Individual experiences vary widely, and no outcome described or implied in this book is guaranteed.

The author does not claim that mutation is superior to growth, nor that growth is inherently flawed. The phrase *"Don't Grow—Mutate"* is a philosophical provocation, not a universal rule. It challenges conventional narratives of linear self-improvement and invites readers to consider alternative forms of progress that emerge from irregular paths, nonlinear development, and lived experience. Readers are encouraged to engage critically and retain personal agency in deciding what resonates and what does not.

Nothing in this book is intended to encourage harmful behavior, reckless experimentation, self-neglect, or withdrawal from necessary care, support systems, or responsibilities. Any practices, reflections, or exercises described should be approached with self-awareness, personal boundaries, and common sense. If something does not feel safe or appropriate for you, you should not engage with it.

This work reflects the author's perspectives at the time of writing and may include subjective interpretations, symbolic language, and personal philosophies. These views do not represent universal truths, scientific consensus, or institutional positions. The author assumes no responsibility for how readers choose to interpret or apply the material.

By reading this book, you acknowledge that you are solely responsible for your choices, actions, interpretations, and outcomes. The author and publisher disclaim any liability for direct or indirect consequences arising from the use or misuse of the content within this work.

This book is an invitation—not a prescription.

Read it as reflection, not instruction.

Use it as a mirror, not a mandate.

Introduction: Mutation over Motivation — Why This Is the New Mode

Motivation is a fragile fuel.

It depends on mood, belief, reward, approval, energy, hope. It asks you to *feel* ready before you move. It assumes a stable body, a cooperative mind, a supportive environment, and a future that responds proportionally to effort. It works best in clean systems—classrooms, offices, gym ads, productivity blogs—where progress is linear and failure is temporary.

But most lives are not clean systems.

Most lives are pressure chambers.

Pain doesn't wait for motivation. Scarcity doesn't ask if you're inspired. Illness, trauma, disability, grief, poverty, betrayal, and exhaustion don't pause until you feel aligned. In those conditions, motivation collapses. It flickers. It lies. It turns into shame: *Why can't I just push harder? Why doesn't this work for me?*

This book begins with a refusal.

Not a refusal to grow—but a refusal to pretend that growth is always the right model.

Growth implies symmetry.
Growth implies order.
Growth implies that the system works.

Mutation does not.

Mutation is what happens when survival precedes belief. When adaptation occurs without permission. When the environment becomes hostile and the organism changes anyway—not neatly, not optimally, but *enough*.

Mutation is not pretty. It is not motivational. It does not announce itself with affirmations or morning routines. It happens quietly, under stress, under constraint, under damage. It is uneven. It produces asymmetry, strange strengths, unexpected capacities, and forms that don't fit the original blueprint.

And yet—mutation works.

Where motivation fails under pressure, mutation persists. Where inspiration burns out, mutation endures. Where "self-improvement" breaks, mutation adapts.

This is why mutation is the new mode.

The Collapse of Motivation Culture

Modern motivation culture sells a fantasy: that effort plus belief equals success. That discipline fixes everything. That consistency is available to everyone equally. That if you are not progressing, you are not trying hard enough—or not wanting it badly enough.

This narrative quietly excludes millions of people.

It excludes those whose nervous systems are overloaded.

Those whose bodies don't reset overnight.

Those whose lives are interrupted by caregiving, illness, bureaucracy, violence, instability, or survival labor.

Those whose minds are fractured not by laziness, but by constant threat.

Motivation culture does not account for broken environments. It assumes the system is neutral and the individual is the variable. When progress stalls, it blames the person—not the conditions.

Mutation flips this logic.

Mutation assumes the environment is hostile by default. It does not ask how to optimize performance within the system—it asks how to *change shape* to survive the system.

Motivation says: *Try harder.*

Mutation says: *Become different.*

Motivation says: *Stay consistent.*

Mutation says: *Stay alive.*

Motivation demands willpower.

Mutation generates capacity.

Why Growth Is No Longer Enough

Growth is linear. It moves upward, outward, forward. It expects continuity. It expects accumulation. It expects yesterday's tools to work tomorrow.

But many lives do not move linearly. They loop. They stall. They regress. They fracture. They are interrupted by events that permanently alter capacity, access, and identity.

In those lives, growth becomes cruel.

Growth tells you to return to who you were before the injury.
Mutation accepts that the old form is gone.

Growth tells you to rebuild the same structure stronger.
Mutation asks whether that structure ever served you.

Growth insists on coherence.
Mutation allows contradiction.

Growth asks you to scale.
Mutation asks you to adapt.

This book is not anti-growth. It is post-growth.

It recognizes that some transformations are not improvements of the old self, but the emergence of something else entirely.

Mutation as Intelligence, Not Failure

Mutation has been framed as defect, error, deviation.

This is a lie born of comfort.

In reality, mutation is intelligence under constraint. It is what systems do when standard pathways are blocked. It is not chosen—it is *generated*. It does not wait for clarity—it responds to pressure.

In human terms, mutation looks like:

- Building strange skills because normal ones were unavailable
- Creating value in ways that don't resemble accepted success
- Learning endurance instead of motivation
- Developing intuition where structure failed
- Becoming asymmetric, nonlinear, unconventional—and functional

Mutation does not care if it looks impressive.

It cares if it works.

This book treats mutation not as pathology, but as a valid mode of becoming—especially for those whose lives have already diverged from the standard path.

Why This Book Exists

This book was not written to motivate you.

It was written because motivation is not enough—and for many people, it never was.

It was written for those who have already tried the systems and failed through no fault of their own. For those whose bodies, minds, circumstances, or histories do not respond to motivational pressure. For those who feel broken by advice that assumes they are intact.

It was written to offer a different operating logic.

One that does not require belief before action.

One that does not demand consistency before capacity.

One that does not punish deviation.

Mutation does not ask you to become better.

It asks you to become *viable*.

The Shift in Mode

This is a shift from:

- Inspiration → adaptation
- Willpower → structural change
- Identity goals → functional outcomes
- Motivation cycles → survival systems
- Growth narratives → mutation logic

It is not louder. It is not cleaner. It is not inspirational in the traditional sense.

It is effective.

And in a world that increasingly breaks people while demanding performance, effectiveness—not motivation—is the real revolution.

What You Are Being Invited Into

This book does not promise transformation through positivity. It does not offer hacks, routines, or aestheticized struggle. It does not guarantee success, happiness, or clarity.

It offers a reframing.

If growth has failed you, you are not defective. If motivation has abandoned you, you are not weak. If your path looks wrong, irregular, or unrecognizable—it may be *mutational*, not broken.

You are not behind.

You are changing shape.

And in this era, that may be the most intelligent thing you can do.

Chapter 1: The Growth Lie

Growth Was Never Neutral

Growth has always been framed as natural, inevitable, and universally good. From childhood onward, we are taught that to grow is to succeed—that upward movement is proof of health, intelligence, and worth. Charts rise. Grades improve. Bodies develop. Careers advance. The implication is subtle but constant: if you are not growing, something is wrong with you.

What is rarely acknowledged is that growth is not a neutral process. It assumes stable conditions. It assumes access to resources. It assumes time, safety, energy, and continuity. Growth thrives in environments where nourishment is predictable and damage is minimal. When those conditions disappear, growth doesn't become harder—it becomes irrelevant.

The lie begins when growth is treated as a moral requirement rather than a situational outcome. When progress stalls, the blame is placed on the individual rather than the environment. You are told to be more disciplined, more positive, more committed—never to question whether the conditions themselves are incompatible with growth.

Growth culture quietly erases disruption. It has no language for chronic interruption, systemic pressure, or long-term instability. It does not know what to do with bodies that don't recover, minds that don't reset, or lives that cannot be paused and optimized. Instead, it labels these realities as personal failures.

This is where the lie becomes harmful. Growth stops being a description of change and becomes a judgment. Those who cannot grow on schedule are seen as stagnant, lazy, or broken. The truth is simpler and harsher: growth is conditional, and those conditions are not evenly distributed.

Linear Progress Is a Fairytale

Linear progress is one of the most seductive myths of modern life. It promises that effort accumulates cleanly—that today builds on yesterday, and tomorrow will reward consistency. This model works well in controlled environments: classrooms, training programs, corporate ladders. It fails almost everywhere else.

Real lives do not move in straight lines. They loop, collapse, restart, and stall. Health fluctuates. Resources vanish. Responsibilities multiply. Trauma interrupts memory, focus, and energy. Linear progress has no answer for these realities except guilt.

When linearity is treated as the default, deviation feels like regression. Rest feels like failure. Survival feels like underachievement. People internalize the belief that if they are not advancing, they are falling behind—even when they are holding their lives together under extraordinary pressure.

This belief creates a constant sense of being late to one's own life. You are always catching up, always behind some invisible schedule. The goalposts move, but the shame remains. Linear progress becomes a weapon used against those whose lives are nonlinear by necessity.

Mutation rejects linearity entirely. It recognizes that adaptation does not follow straight paths. It accepts that change can be sideways, uneven, and discontinuous—and still be real. Progress does not have to look like ascent to be valid.

Motivation Was Built for Stable Lives

Motivation is marketed as a universal tool, but it was designed for a very specific kind of life: one with predictability, support, and margin. Motivation assumes that energy replenishes, that effort leads to reward, and that setbacks are temporary.

For unstable lives, motivation becomes unreliable at best and cruel at worst. When your nervous system is overloaded, motivation does not rise—it drains. When your body is managing pain or fatigue, motivation does not respond to slogans. When survival tasks consume your day, motivation becomes an abstract luxury.

The problem is not a lack of desire. Most people want stability, dignity, and relief. The problem is that motivation requires surplus—surplus energy, surplus hope, surplus safety. Without surplus, motivation collapses under its own weight.

Growth culture treats this collapse as a character flaw. It tells you to push through exhaustion, to override limits, to discipline yourself harder. In doing so, it ignores the signals that adaptation—not effort—is required.

Mutation does not depend on motivation. It emerges from necessity. It operates even when belief is gone. It is not fueled by inspiration but by pressure, constraint, and the refusal to disappear. That is why it works where motivation fails.

The Productivity Trap

Productivity has become the visible metric of growth. Output is mistaken for progress. Busyness is confused with value. If you are producing, you are seen as moving forward—regardless of cost.

This trap is especially dangerous for those whose lives already demand constant labor just to maintain baseline functioning. Caregiving, managing illness, navigating systems, and emotional regulation are invisible forms of work. They consume time and energy but produce nothing that growth culture recognizes.

As a result, people are told they are unproductive while they are exhausted from surviving. They are encouraged to add more tasks, optimize routines, and squeeze efficiency from already depleted reserves. Burnout is reframed as a mindset issue rather than a structural one.

Productivity culture does not ask whether the output is sustainable. It does not care if the system breaks the person, as long as the metrics improve. Growth becomes extraction—taking more from the individual than the environment gives back.

Mutation refuses extraction. It prioritizes viability over output. It asks not "How much can you produce?" but "What allows you to continue?" This shift alone dismantles the productivity trap.

Growth Punishes the Already Altered

Growth narratives are built around the idea of returning to form—getting back on track, bouncing back, reclaiming your former self. For those whose bodies, minds, or lives have been permanently altered, this narrative is devastating.

Disability, trauma, chronic illness, and long-term instability change the baseline. There is no "before" to return to. Growth culture treats this reality as temporary denial rather than permanent context. It insists on restoration where adaptation is required.

This creates a constant tension between who you are and who you are told you should be. The effort to reconcile the two becomes exhausting. You are always failing to meet an image that no longer fits your reality.

Mutation accepts alteration as fact, not failure. It does not attempt to restore what was lost. It builds from what exists now. It treats difference as data rather than deficit.

For the already altered, mutation is not a choice—it is the only honest path forward. Growth demands conformity. Mutation allows divergence.

Why the Lie Persists

The growth lie persists because it benefits systems more than people. Linear progress is easy to measure. Motivation is easy to commodify. Productivity is easy to extract. These frameworks create predictable outputs and manageable narratives.

Mutation, by contrast, is messy. It resists standardization. It produces outcomes that do not fit neat categories. It cannot be easily packaged, sold, or scaled. Systems that depend on uniform performance have no incentive to validate it.

As a result, mutation is reframed as dysfunction. Adaptation is mislabeled as inconsistency. Survival strategies are called bad habits. People are pressured to abandon what keeps them alive in favor of what looks correct.

This chapter exists to name the lie plainly. Growth is not wrong—but it is not universal. When conditions break, growth models fail. Pretending otherwise only deepens harm.

Mutation is not a rejection of progress. It is a refusal to sacrifice viability for appearances. And once you see the lie, you cannot unsee it.

Exercises

Exercise 1: Identifying the Growth Script

1. Write down three messages you've internalized about growth (e.g., "I should be further along by now").
2. For each message, identify where it came from (school, family, work, culture).
3. Write one sentence describing how this message has made you feel when you couldn't meet it.
4. Ask: *Does this message account for my actual conditions?*
5. Rewrite the message in a way that acknowledges reality instead of denying it.

Exercise 2: Mapping Nonlinear Change

1. Draw a rough timeline of the last five years of your life.
2. Mark major disruptions, pauses, or reversals.
3. Next to each, write one adaptation you developed—even if it felt small or unwanted.
4. Identify one strength that exists now that did not exist before those disruptions.
5. Sit with the idea that this is change, even if it wasn't growth.

Exercise 3: Viability Check

1. Choose one area of your life where you feel "behind."
2. List what growth culture says you *should* be doing there.
3. List what you are actually capable of right now.
4. Identify one adjustment that would make the situation more livable rather than more impressive.
5. Commit to that adjustment for one week.

Journal Prompts

1. When did I first learn that growth equals worth?
2. Where has linear progress failed to describe my life accurately?
3. What has survival taught me that growth never could?
4. In what ways has motivation been unreliable for me—and why?
5. What kinds of effort go unseen in my daily life?
6. How has productivity culture distorted my sense of value?
7. What part of me has been labeled "stuck" that was actually adapting?
8. What am I tired of trying to return to?
9. What does viability mean to me right now?
10. If growth were optional, what would I allow myself to become?

Closing Reflection

Growth promised clarity, direction, and reward—but only under conditions that were never guaranteed. When those conditions disappeared, the promise turned into pressure. This chapter is not an argument against improvement; it is an invitation to stop measuring yourself by a model that cannot account for your reality.

You are not failing at growth.

You are responding to conditions growth was never designed to survive.

Mutation begins where the lie ends.

Chapter 2: Mutation as Method

Mutation Is Not Chaos

Mutation is often misunderstood as randomness—an uncontrolled deviation from the norm. This misunderstanding comes from comparing mutation to planning, as if change must always be intentional to be valid. In reality, mutation is not chaos; it is response. It is patterned adaptation under pressure, shaped by constraints rather than ideals.

Unlike motivation-driven change, mutation does not begin with a goal. It begins with a condition. Something no longer works. A pathway closes. Energy drops. Time collapses. The system—your body, mind, or life—adjusts because it must. The adjustment may not be elegant, but it is functional.

Chaos implies lack of intelligence. Mutation is intelligence expressed without permission. It is the body compensating when the mind is exhausted. It is the mind rerouting when the body cannot comply. It is the self becoming something else because remaining the same would be lethal or unsustainable.

This is why mutation is reliable under pressure. It does not wait for clarity or confidence. It responds to friction. It builds workarounds instead of fantasies. It does not ask what should happen—it asks what *can* happen.

As a method, mutation is not about controlling outcomes. It is about noticing adaptations already occurring and reinforcing the ones that increase viability. You are not inventing change from scratch. You are learning how to recognize and work with the changes already underway.

From Identity to Function

Growth culture prioritizes identity: who you are becoming, how you see yourself, what label fits your trajectory. Mutation bypasses identity and moves directly to function. It asks one question repeatedly: *What works now?*

When identity leads, change becomes fragile. If you cannot act in alignment with who you think you should be, shame follows. You feel inconsistent, inauthentic, or broken. Identity-based change collapses the moment reality disrupts self-image.

Mutation does not require coherence. You can contradict yourself and still adapt. You can change strategies without rewriting your identity. You can abandon methods without abandoning yourself. Function matters more than narrative.

This shift is liberating for those whose lives do not allow consistency. You do not need to "become" disciplined to create structure. You do not need to "believe" in yourself to build capacity. You do not need to identify as strong to endure.

Mutation replaces identity questions with functional ones. Not *Who am I becoming?* but *What keeps me going?* Not *What does this say about me?* but *Does this reduce harm or increase stability?* These questions are survivable even on bad days.

Constraint Is the Engine

Motivation assumes abundance. Mutation assumes constraint. This is not pessimism—it is realism. Most people operate under limits: limited energy, limited time, limited money, limited support. Ignoring these limits does not make them disappear; it makes adaptation harder.

Constraint is not the enemy of change—it is the engine of it. When resources are scarce, systems become efficient. When pathways close, alternatives emerge. When capacity drops, prioritization sharpens. Constraint forces intelligence.

Growth culture treats constraint as an obstacle to overcome. Mutation treats it as data. Instead of asking how to eliminate limits, mutation asks how to work *with* them. This prevents self-betrayal and burnout.

This does not mean accepting harm or settling for less. It means designing change that respects reality. A system that ignores constraints will eventually collapse. A system built around them can endure.

Mutation as method begins with mapping constraints honestly. Not to shame yourself—but to stop fighting conditions you cannot change and start shaping responses you can sustain.

Adaptation Over Optimization

Optimization promises efficiency, performance, and peak output. It assumes a stable system that can be fine-tuned indefinitely. For unstable lives, optimization becomes a trap. There is nothing to optimize when the system itself is under threat.

Adaptation is different. It does not seek peak performance. It seeks survivability. It prioritizes flexibility over efficiency and redundancy over elegance. An adaptive system may look inefficient from the outside—but it keeps functioning when conditions worsen.

Optimization asks: *How can I do this better?*

Adaptation asks: *How can I keep doing this at all?*

This distinction matters. Many people burn out trying to optimize lives that require adaptation. They chase routines, hacks, and systems that assume consistency they do not have. When those systems fail, they blame themselves instead of the mismatch.

Mutation favors adaptive strategies: uneven pacing, modular habits, fallback plans, partial successes. These approaches do not impress productivity culture, but they work under stress.

As a method, mutation rejects perfection. It values durability. If something works 40% of the time under bad conditions, it may be more valuable than something that works 100% of the time only when everything is ideal.

Reinforcing Useful Mutations

You are already mutating. This is not theoretical. You have already developed workarounds, compensations, and strategies to survive your life. The mistake is ignoring these adaptations because they don't look like growth.

Mutation as method means identifying which adaptations increase viability and reinforcing them deliberately. This is not about adding more effort—it is about directing attention.

Some mutations reduce harm: pacing yourself, avoiding certain environments, lowering expectations strategically. Others increase capacity: unconventional scheduling, niche skills, asymmetric strengths. Some do both.

Growth culture pressures you to abandon these strategies in favor of "better" ones. Mutation asks whether abandoning them would make your life harder. If the answer is yes, the strategy deserves respect.

Reinforcement does not mean overuse. It means recognizing value. It means refining what already works instead of forcing alignment with external models.

This is how mutation becomes method: by treating adaptation as legitimate, intentional, and worthy of cultivation.

Living Systems, Not Life Plans

Life plans assume predictability. They rely on forecasts, timelines, and milestones. When disruption occurs, the plan breaks—and often, so does the person trying to follow it.

Living systems operate differently. They respond continuously to feedback. They adjust without needing to justify change. They are not committed to a single outcome, only to continued viability.

Mutation aligns with systems thinking rather than goal obsession. It allows direction without rigidity. It supports movement without requiring certainty.

This does not mean drifting aimlessly. It means holding direction lightly and responding honestly. A living system can change shape without losing coherence.

As a method, mutation invites you to stop treating your life as a project to be completed and start treating it as a system to be maintained. Maintenance is not failure. It is intelligence expressed over time.

Exercises

Exercise 1: Mutation Inventory

1. List five ways you currently cope, adapt, or compensate in daily life.
2. For each, note whether it reduces harm, increases capacity, or both.
3. Identify one adaptation you've been ashamed of or dismissed.
4. Ask: *What problem does this actually solve?*
5. Decide whether this adaptation deserves reinforcement rather than removal.

Exercise 2: Constraint Mapping

1. Choose one area of your life that feels difficult to "improve."
2. List all current constraints affecting it (energy, time, money, health, support).
3. Circle the constraints that are unlikely to change soon.
4. Brainstorm one adjustment that works *within* those constraints.
5. Implement that adjustment for one week without trying to optimize it.

Exercise 3: Function First Design

1. Pick one recurring task or responsibility.
2. Write down how you think it *should* be done.
3. Write down how you actually do it.
4. Identify which version is more sustainable under stress.
5. Modify the task to prioritize completion over perfection.

Journal Prompts

1. Where has adaptation already saved me?
2. What strategies have I judged unfairly because they didn't look impressive?
3. How do constraints shape my intelligence rather than limit it?
4. When has optimization made my life harder instead of easier?
5. What does "working" actually mean for me right now?
6. How does my body already communicate necessary change?
7. What would I stop forcing if function mattered more than image?
8. Where am I already different from the expected path?
9. What kind of system does my life actually require?
10. How might I cooperate with change instead of managing it?

Closing Reflection

Mutation does not ask you to rise above your conditions.
It asks you to respond honestly to them.

As a method, mutation replaces aspiration with awareness and force with flexibility. It does not promise improvement—it offers continuity. In a world that breaks plans faster than people can make them, continuity is not small.

You do not need a better mindset.
You need a system that can survive your reality.

Mutation is not what happens when you fail to grow.
It is what happens when you learn how to live.

Chapter 3: Breaking Human Templates

The Myth of the Default Human

There is an unspoken assumption baked into nearly every system you interact with: that there is a "default" human. This default human wakes up rested, has consistent energy, regulates emotions predictably, learns linearly, recovers quickly, and responds well to motivation and structure. Most advice, policies, and expectations are built around this figure.

The problem is not that this template exists—it's that it's treated as universal. When systems fail people, the failure is attributed to deviation from the template rather than flaws in the template itself. You are told to adjust yourself to fit the mold, even when the mold was never designed for you.

This creates a quiet violence. People internalize the belief that their struggles are personal malfunctions instead of mismatches. The question becomes "What's wrong with me?" instead of "Who was this built for?"

The default human is not a neutral average. It is an idealized composite shaped by privilege, health, stability, and predictability. Treating it as standard erases the vast range of real human variation.

Breaking human templates begins by recognizing that you were never failing to be human—you were failing to conform to an abstraction that was never meant to include you.

Templates Are Tools, Not Truths

Templates are useful until they aren't. They simplify complexity, reduce uncertainty, and create shared expectations. In controlled environments, this can be efficient. In lived reality, templates often outlive their usefulness.

The mistake is mistaking tools for truths. A template is a model, not a mandate. It is a rough approximation, not a moral standard. When it stops working, clinging to it becomes self-destructive.

Human templates are particularly dangerous because they disguise themselves as nature. Phrases like "everyone can," "this is normal," and "you just have to" hide design assumptions behind inevitability. They imply that deviation is unnatural rather than expected.

Mutation exposes the truth: templates are conditional. They work for some people in some contexts for some time. Outside those conditions, they fail—and they should be discarded without shame.

Breaking a template is not rebellion. It is maintenance. It is recognizing when a model no longer fits the system it's applied to and choosing function over conformity.

Normalization as Control

Normalization is often framed as inclusion—bringing people into the fold, helping them meet standards, offering support to "catch up." But normalization is also a form of control. It defines what counts as acceptable before offering help.

Support is frequently conditional: you are helped as long as you move toward normal. Accommodations are temporary. Patience expires. The expectation is always eventual alignment with the template.

This creates pressure to perform normalcy rather than build viability. People hide symptoms, suppress needs, and exhaust themselves to appear functional. The cost is paid privately while compliance is rewarded publicly.

Normalization rewards those who can approximate the template and punishes those who cannot. It treats difference as a problem to be fixed rather than a signal that the system needs adjustment.

Mutation rejects normalization as the end goal. It does not aim to make you legible to systems that erase you. It prioritizes survival, sustainability, and coherence on your own terms—even if that coherence looks unfamiliar.

When the Body Refuses the Script

The body is often the first to reject a template. Fatigue, pain, dissociation, sensory overload, and shutdown are not moral failures—they are refusals. They are the body communicating that the script is incompatible with reality.

Growth culture interprets these signals as obstacles to overcome. Push through. Retrain your habits. Optimize your sleep. Discipline your mind. The assumption is that the body must be corrected to resume compliance.

Mutation listens instead. It treats bodily resistance as information. If the body will not perform, the template—not the body—comes into question.

This reframing is radical. It removes blame and introduces curiosity. Instead of asking how to force capacity, mutation asks how to redesign expectations. Instead of demanding endurance, it explores pacing, rerouting, and substitution.

Breaking human templates requires trusting the body as a diagnostic tool. Not everything that hurts needs to be healed. Some things hurt because they are wrong for you.

Designing for the Outliers

Outliers are treated as edge cases—exceptions to be managed rather than signals to be studied. Yet history shows that designing for outliers often produces better systems for everyone.

When you design for those with limited energy, everyone benefits from efficiency. When you design for those with sensory sensitivity, environments become calmer. When you design for unpredictability, systems become resilient.

Mutation aligns with outlier-first design. It does not ask how to bring the outlier into the center—it asks how to redesign the center to accommodate reality.

This approach validates difference without requiring assimilation. It allows people to stop translating themselves constantly. It reduces the friction of existing in systems that were never meant to hold you.

Breaking templates is not about isolation. It is about expanding what counts as functional, human, and valid.

Becoming Untemplated

To become untemplated is not to reject structure entirely. It is to stop outsourcing self-definition to models that erase your reality. It is to choose alignment over approval.

This process can feel destabilizing. Templates offer certainty, even when they harm. Letting go of them can feel like losing direction. Mutation replaces that false certainty with responsiveness.

An untemplated life is not chaotic—it is adaptive. It responds to feedback instead of enforcing expectations. It evolves without apology.

You are allowed to build a life that does not resemble the brochure. You are allowed to function differently. You are allowed to stop trying to pass as someone you are not.

Breaking human templates is not the end of becoming. It is the beginning of coherence.

Exercises

Exercise 1: Template Identification

1. List three expectations you feel pressured to meet to be seen as "normal."
2. Identify where each expectation came from (culture, family, work, medicine).
3. Note how your body or life resists each one.
4. Ask: *What breaks when I try to meet this expectation?*
5. Decide whether the template or the expectation deserves to be questioned.

Exercise 2: Body as Feedback

1. Think of a recurring task or role that drains you.
2. Write down the physical or emotional signals that appear when you engage with it.
3. Describe what the template demands in that situation.
4. Imagine redesigning the task to respect the signals instead.
5. Test one small change that honors your body's feedback.

Exercise 3: Untemplated Design

1. Choose one area of life where you feel misaligned.
2. Describe how it would look if designed specifically for you.
3. Remove any requirement to appear normal or impressive.
4. Identify one practical adjustment toward that design.
5. Implement it without explaining or justifying yourself.

Journal Prompts

1. When did I first feel "different" in a way that mattered?
2. Which human template has caused me the most harm?
3. How has normalization disguised control in my life?
4. What signals has my body been sending that I ignored?
5. Where am I performing normalcy at my own expense?
6. What would it mean to trust my difference?
7. How has being an outlier sharpened my intelligence?
8. What systems was I never meant to fit into?
9. What does an untemplated life feel like in my body?
10. If no one were watching, how would I function differently?

Closing Reflection

Templates promise belonging—but only to those who can afford conformity. When you break them, you are not rejecting humanity. You are reclaiming it.

You do not need to become more normal.
You need to become more *true to your conditions*.

Mutation does not flatten difference.
It lets difference become form.

And once the template breaks, you are finally free to exist without translation.

Chapter 4: Weaponized Becoming

When Change Is No Longer Innocent

Becoming is often framed as a gentle process—self-discovery, growth, healing, evolution. But for many people, becoming was never gentle. It was forced. It was reactive. It was shaped by threat rather than curiosity. This chapter begins by naming a truth most frameworks avoid: change can be weaponized.

Weaponized becoming occurs when adaptation is demanded rather than chosen. When survival requires transformation, but that transformation is judged, monitored, or exploited by others. You are told to change, improve, evolve—yet punished for the very traits that adaptation produces.

In these conditions, becoming stops being about self-expression and starts being about compliance. You learn which versions of yourself are tolerated and which are dangerous. You refine yourself not for coherence, but for safety.

The tragedy is that the skills you develop—hypervigilance, emotional regulation, strategic silence, rapid learning—are powerful. But they are extracted under pressure, without consent, and often without recognition.

Weaponized becoming is not a failure of character. It is what happens when systems demand transformation while refusing to take responsibility for the conditions that made it necessary.

Adaptation Under Surveillance

Surveillance does not always look like cameras or authorities. Often, it looks like evaluation. Performance reviews. Medical assessments. Social judgment. Family scrutiny. Algorithms. Metrics. Expectations that track you constantly.

When adaptation happens under surveillance, it becomes strategic. You learn not just how to change, but how to change *correctly*. You modify behavior to avoid punishment, withdrawal of support, or disbelief. Your becoming becomes legible to power.

This creates a split. There is the version of you that adapts internally—and the version that is allowed to be seen. Over time, maintaining this split consumes enormous energy. Authentic adaptation is hidden. Approved adaptation is displayed.

Growth culture praises this as resilience. In reality, it is a tax. You are paying for survival with invisibility. The more skilled you become, the harder it is for others to believe you are struggling at all.

Mutation acknowledges this dynamic. It recognizes that not all change is safe to reveal. Weaponized becoming teaches discernment—not every adaptation needs to be public to be valid.

Strength That Was Never Meant to Be Yours

Many people carry strengths they never asked for. Crisis management. Emotional containment. Rapid problem-solving. Endurance under pressure. These capacities are often celebrated without acknowledging their origin.

Weaponized becoming produces competence through necessity. You learn because you must. You stabilize because no one else will. You adapt because refusal is not an option. The strength is real—but so is the cost.

Society loves the outcome and ignores the process. You are praised for being capable while denied rest. You are admired for surviving while expected to keep performing. The strength becomes an obligation.

This is how becoming is weaponized against you. The very adaptations that kept you alive are used to justify continued pressure. Your resilience becomes evidence that you don't need relief.

Mutation reframes this entirely. Strength born of harm is not an infinite resource. It deserves context, boundaries, and recovery—not endless extraction.

Reclaiming the Direction of Change

Weaponized becoming strips you of authorship. Change happens *to* you, not *for* you. Reclaiming becoming means reclaiming direction—not by erasing adaptations, but by choosing how they are used.

This requires separating capacity from obligation. Just because you can endure does not mean you should. Just because you adapted once does not mean you owe repetition. Choice is what transforms survival into agency.

Reclamation does not require dismantling everything at once. It begins with selective refusal. You stop offering your adaptations automatically. You decide where your strength is spent.

Mutation supports this shift. It treats becoming as a resource that belongs to you. Adaptations can be repurposed, redirected, or retired. You are allowed to change how you change.

Weaponized becoming loses power the moment authorship returns.

Turning the Weapon Inward—And Why It Fails

Many people internalize weaponized becoming. They use their own adaptations against themselves. They demand constant improvement. They punish rest. They equate stagnation with danger.

This internalization feels like discipline, but it is actually fear. The fear that if you stop adapting, everything collapses. That if you rest, you lose value. That safety is conditional on performance.

The problem is that this strategy worked once—but it does not scale indefinitely. What saved you under threat will destroy you in stability. The weapon turns inward, eroding capacity instead of protecting it.

Mutation recognizes when a tool has outlived its context. It allows you to retire strategies that were useful but are now harmful. This is not regression—it is intelligence updating itself.

You do not have to remain in emergency mode to justify your existence.

Becoming as a Controlled Burn

Reclaimed becoming is not passive. It is intentional, bounded, and strategic. It is a controlled burn rather than a wildfire—change that is directed instead of reactive.

This kind of becoming respects limits. It includes rest as a component, not a reward. It allows pauses without interpreting them as danger. It honors the fact that not all change must be visible or productive.

Weaponized becoming thrives on urgency. Reclaimed becoming moves at a pace that sustains you. It does not exist to impress systems or satisfy metrics.

This is where mutation matures. It stops being pure reaction and becomes method with boundaries. You still adapt—but you choose when, how, and why.

Becoming is no longer something done *to* you. It becomes something you wield carefully—on your own terms.

Exercises

Exercise 1: Mapping Weaponized Change

1. Identify one way you were forced to adapt to survive.
2. Write down what skill or strength emerged from that adaptation.
3. Note who benefited most from that strength—then and now.
4. Ask: *Do I still consent to using this adaptation in the same way?*
5. Decide one boundary around how this strength is used going forward.

Exercise 2: Capacity vs. Obligation

1. List three things you are "good at" because you had to be.
2. Next to each, write whether it currently serves or drains you.
3. Identify one place you feel obligated to perform this strength.
4. Imagine withdrawing or limiting it safely.
5. Take one small step toward reducing automatic performance.

Exercise 3: Controlled Burn Design

1. Choose one area where you are pushing too hard.
2. Identify the fear driving that pressure.
3. Define what *enough* would look like instead of more.
4. Build in one intentional pause or limit.
5. Observe what happens when urgency is reduced.

Journal Prompts

1. When did becoming stop feeling like a choice for me?
2. What strengths do I carry that came from pressure or harm?
3. How has my adaptability been used against me?
4. Where do I confuse endurance with worth?
5. What adaptations am I afraid to let go of—and why?
6. How do I punish myself for resting?
7. What would authorship over my change look like?
8. Where does urgency still control me?
9. What kind of becoming would feel humane?
10. How can I protect my adaptations instead of offering them up?

Closing Reflection

You were never wrong for becoming what you needed to survive. But survival strategies are not life sentences.

Weaponized becoming teaches you how powerful you are— Reclaimed becoming teaches you how to stop paying for that power with yourself.

Change does not have to be violent to be real. And becoming does not have to be a battlefield.

When authorship returns, mutation stops being a weapon— and becomes a tool you finally control.

Chapter 5: Mutation Without Apology

The Demand to Explain Yourself

Most people are not punished for changing—they are punished for changing *without permission*. The demand rarely comes as a direct command. It arrives as questions: *Why are you doing it this way? Have you tried...? Is that really necessary?* These questions masquerade as concern while quietly enforcing conformity.

Explanation becomes the toll you are expected to pay for divergence. The more your life deviates from the expected path, the more justification is required. You are asked to translate your reality into language that reassures others you are still understandable, still compliant, still safe.

This demand drains energy. It forces you to relive decisions, defend adaptations, and prove necessity. Over time, you begin to preemptively justify yourself—even when no one is asking. Apology becomes reflex.

Mutation without apology begins by recognizing this pattern as external control. You are not required to make your survival strategies legible to everyone. Understanding is not a prerequisite for validity.

Refusing to explain is not hostility. It is conservation. It is choosing to spend energy on living rather than narrating your right to exist.

Legibility Is Not the Same as Health

Legibility is often mistaken for wellness. When others can easily understand your behavior, routine, or choices, they assume you are doing well. When they cannot, concern—or correction—follows.

But legibility serves systems, not bodies. Systems require predictability. They reward those who move in recognizable ways. Health, by contrast, is often idiosyncratic. What stabilizes one person may destabilize another.

Mutation produces forms that are hard to read. Asymmetrical schedules. Unconventional priorities. Selective participation. These choices may look dysfunctional from the outside while being essential internally.

Apology creeps in when you confuse misunderstanding with wrongdoing. You begin to smooth edges, perform coherence, and suppress adaptations that actually work—just to remain legible.

Mutation without apology rejects this trade. You are allowed to be opaque. You are allowed to function in ways that don't translate cleanly. Health does not require audience approval.

Boundaries That Don't Ask Permission

Boundaries are often taught as polite negotiations. You are encouraged to explain your limits, soften refusals, and reassure others that your boundaries are reasonable. This framing assumes equal power and mutual respect.

In reality, many boundaries exist because respect was absent. They are not requests—they are protections. Requiring justification turns boundaries into debates, and debates invite erosion.

Mutation without apology treats boundaries as statements, not arguments. You do not owe context for limits that exist to keep you functional. The boundary itself is the explanation.

This can feel uncomfortable at first. You may fear being seen as difficult, selfish, or ungrateful. These fears are conditioned responses to systems that benefited from your overextension.

A boundary held without apology is not cruelty. It is clarity. It signals that your capacity is finite and valuable—and that you intend to preserve it.

Letting Go of the Redemption Arc

Many people feel pressure to frame their mutation as a redemption story. If you changed because of pain, you are expected to transform that pain into inspiration. Your suffering must be redeemed through productivity, wisdom, or service.

This narrative is seductive because it promises meaning. But it also traps you in performance. You are never allowed to simply adapt—you must *justify* the adaptation by proving it led to something admirable.

Mutation without apology releases the need for redemption. Not all pain needs a payoff. Not all survival must be aestheticized or instructive. You are not required to turn hardship into a lesson for others.

Letting go of the redemption arc allows honesty. You can acknowledge that some changes were necessary but unwanted. That some adaptations kept you alive but cost you things you still grieve.

You do not owe the world a return on your suffering. Existing without apology is not failure—it is refusal to commodify your own endurance.

Existing Outside the Performance Economy

The performance economy rewards visibility, consistency, and output. It penalizes fluctuation, withdrawal, and maintenance. Within this economy, mutation is tolerated only when it produces marketable results.

Mutation without apology opts out of this logic. It recognizes that not all functioning needs to be optimized, shared, or monetized. Some adaptations exist solely to make life livable.

This does not mean rejecting ambition or creation. It means decoupling worth from constant demonstration. You can build, rest, disappear, and return without narrating the gap.

Performance demands explanation for pauses. Mutation does not. It understands that systems need downtime to recalibrate. Silence is not absence—it is processing.

When you stop performing your survival, you reclaim privacy. When you reclaim privacy, mutation deepens. Not everything that matters needs witnesses.

Standing in Your Shape

To mutate without apology is to stand in your current shape without asking if it's acceptable. This does not mean rigidity. You may change again. You may adapt further. But you do not preemptively shrink to make others comfortable.

Standing in your shape requires tolerating misunderstanding. Some people will not adjust their expectations. Some will withdraw. Some will insist you are doing it wrong.

This is not evidence of failure. It is evidence of divergence. Not everyone can follow you out of the template—and you are not required to bring them.

Mutation without apology is quiet confidence. Not bravado, not defiance—just steadiness. You know what works. You know what it costs to abandon it.

You are allowed to remain in a form that keeps you alive, even if it makes no sense to anyone else.

Exercises

Exercise 1: Apology Audit

1. Notice every time you apologize in a single day.
2. Write down what you apologized for and to whom.
3. Identify which apologies were about harm versus difference.
4. Rewrite one unnecessary apology as a neutral statement.
5. Practice withholding apology in one low-risk situation.

Exercise 2: Boundary Without Backstory

1. Identify one boundary you frequently explain.
2. Write the boundary as a simple statement with no justification.
3. Practice saying it aloud without adding context.
4. Notice any discomfort or urge to soften it.
5. Hold the boundary once without explanation.

Exercise 3: Private Adaptation

1. Choose one adaptation you've been performing publicly.
2. Ask whether sharing it serves you or reassures others.
3. Experiment with keeping it private for one week.
4. Observe any change in energy or clarity.
5. Decide whether this adaptation deserves privacy long-term.

Journal Prompts

1. Where did I learn to apologize for existing differently?
2. What adaptations do I feel pressured to explain?
3. How does legibility cost me energy?
4. What boundaries am I still negotiating instead of holding?
5. Where do I seek redemption for my pain?
6. What would it feel like to stop justifying my survival?
7. How does performance show up in my healing?
8. What parts of my life need privacy to function?
9. Who benefits when I apologize unnecessarily?
10. What does unapologetic existence feel like in my body?

Closing Reflection

Apology is often mistaken for humility.
In reality, it is frequently a response to pressure—not wrongdoing.

You do not need permission to adapt.
You do not need approval to remain viable.
You do not need to explain the shape that keeps you alive.

Mutation without apology is not arrogance.
It is acceptance—without negotiation.

You are allowed to exist in your form
without translating it, redeeming it, or defending it.

This is not defiance.
This is self-respect, finally practiced.

Appendix A: Mutation Sequence Blueprint

This appendix is not a motivational roadmap.
It is not a promise of progress, healing, or arrival.

It is a **functional blueprint**—a repeatable sequence for navigating change when growth models fail, motivation collapses, and identity-based frameworks become liabilities.

Mutation is not a moment.
It is a **process that unfolds in phases**, often cyclically, often unevenly. These phases do not move cleanly forward. They loop, overlap, stall, and restart. That is not error—it is design.

What follows is a **mutation sequence** you can return to whenever conditions change, capacity drops, or survival demands adaptation.

Phase One: Environmental Pressure Recognition

Mutation never begins with desire.
It begins with **pressure**.

This pressure may appear as exhaustion, stagnation, repeated failure, bodily resistance, emotional shutdown, or the sense that familiar strategies no longer work. The mistake most people make is treating this moment as personal deficiency instead of environmental signal.

This phase requires **honest recognition**:

- Something about your current conditions is incompatible with your existing form.
- Effort is no longer producing proportional return.
- The cost of maintaining normalcy exceeds its benefit.

At this stage, most systems push you toward motivation: *try harder, recommit, reframe*. Mutation rejects this reflex. Pressure is not a cue to intensify effort—it is a cue to reassess structure.

Key markers of this phase:

- Chronic friction rather than temporary difficulty
- Repeated burnout or collapse after "getting back on track"
- Bodily refusal (fatigue, pain, dissociation, shutdown)
- Loss of belief in familiar narratives of success

This phase is diagnostic, not actionable.
Do not rush it.
Misreading pressure leads to self-violence.

Phase Two: Growth Model Failure Acknowledgment

Once pressure is recognized, the next step is to **explicitly name what no longer works.**

This phase is about identifying the *model* that failed—not blaming yourself for failing within it.

Growth models that commonly collapse include:

- Linear progress expectations
- Motivation-based discipline
- Identity-driven consistency
- Productivity-as-worth
- Normalization frameworks

The danger here is nostalgia. Many people cling to broken models because they once worked—or worked for others. This creates repeated self-abandonment.

Acknowledgment requires precision:

- What strategy failed?
- Under what conditions?
- At what cost?

This is not about erasing the past. It is about recognizing that **context has changed**, and the model did not adapt with it.

If you skip this phase, you will attempt mutation while secretly trying to return to growth—creating internal conflict and self-doubt.

Phase Three: Constraint Mapping

Mutation does not ignore limits.
It begins by **mapping them accurately**.

Constraints are not weaknesses. They are the terrain. Mutation designs *with* terrain, not against it.

Common constraint categories:

- Energy (physical, neurological, emotional)
- Time (interruptions, caregiving, instability)
- Resources (money, access, support)
- Capacity (health, cognition, mobility)
- Safety (emotional, relational, systemic)

This phase demands ruthless honesty. Inflating capacity leads to collapse. Underestimating capacity leads to unnecessary restriction. The goal is accuracy.

Ask:

- What is consistently limited right now?
- What fluctuates?
- What is non-negotiable?

Mutation only becomes sustainable when it stops pretending capacity is stable.

Phase Four: Emergent Adaptation Identification

You are not starting from zero.
You are already adapting.

This phase focuses on **surfacing existing mutations**—strategies you developed informally to survive pressure.

These may include:

- Unconventional schedules
- Selective engagement or withdrawal
- Asymmetric skill development
- Lowered expectations in specific domains
- Avoidance of certain environments or people

Growth culture labels these as failures, bad habits, or avoidance. Mutation reframes them as **data**.

The question is not *"Is this ideal?"*
The question is *"What problem does this solve?"*

Some adaptations reduce harm.
Some increase capacity.
Some do both.

This phase is about recognition, not endorsement. You cannot refine what you refuse to acknowledge.

Phase Five: Functional Reinforcement

Not all adaptations should be kept—but some should be strengthened.

In this phase, you:

- Select adaptations that improve viability
- Remove moral judgment
- Reinforce them deliberately

Reinforcement may look like:

- Formalizing an informal workaround
- Protecting an adaptation with boundaries
- Designing systems that support it
- Letting go of shame around it

This is where mutation becomes **method** instead of reaction.

Importantly, reinforcement is not escalation. You do not push the adaptation harder—you **support it structurally** so it costs less to maintain.

Phase Six: Boundary Establishment

Mutation without boundaries becomes extraction.

Once adaptations increase capacity, systems—people, institutions, expectations—often respond by demanding more. This is where weaponized becoming reappears.

This phase establishes **non-negotiable limits**:

- Where adaptation is offered
- Where it is withheld
- Where performance stops

Boundaries at this stage are not negotiable or explanatory. They exist to preserve the mutation itself.

If a boundary threatens collapse when enforced, it was needed sooner.

Phase Seven: Apology Elimination

This phase removes **excess justification**.

Apologies are appropriate for harm—not for difference. Mutation often triggers apology reflexes because it disrupts expectation.

Here, you:

- Stop narrating your survival
- Reduce explanations to the minimum necessary
- Allow misunderstanding without correction

This is not confrontation.
It is **energy conservation**.

Mutation stabilizes when it no longer requires translation.

Phase Eight: Iterative Reassessment

Mutation is not permanent form—it is **ongoing response.**

This phase loops you back to the beginning, not as failure but as maintenance.

Ask periodically:

- Has pressure changed?
- Have constraints shifted?
- Are adaptations still functional?
- Have boundaries held?

Mutation sequences repeat at new scales. What worked last year may fail next year. That does not invalidate the method—it confirms its necessity.

Using the Blueprint

This blueprint is not meant to be completed once.
It is meant to be **returned to**.

Use it when:

- You hit burnout again
- A system collapses
- Capacity changes suddenly
- Motivation disappears
- Growth advice starts harming you

You do not need all phases at once.
You may be living in one phase for months.

Mutation does not reward speed.
It rewards accuracy.

Final Note

Growth asks you to become more of what you already were.
Mutation allows you to become **something else entirely**—without apology, without justification, without collapse.

This blueprint does not promise success.
It promises **continuation**.

And for many lives, continuation is not a small thing.

Message from the Author:

I hope you enjoyed this book, I love astrology and knew there was not a book such as this out on the shelf. I love metaphysical items as well. Please check out my other books:

-Life of Government Benefits

-My life of Hell

-My life with Hydrocephalus

-Red Sky

-World Domination:Woman's rule

-World Domination:Woman's Rule 2: The War

-Life and Banishment of Apophis: book 1

-The Kidney Friendly Diet

-The Ultimate Hemp Cookbook

-Creating a Dispensary(legally)

-Cleanliness throughout life: the importance of showering from childhood to adulthood.

-Strong Roots: The Risks of Overcoddling children

-Hemp Horoscopes: Cosmic Insights and Earthly Healing

- Celestial Hemp Navigating the Zodiac: Through the Green Cosmos

-Astrological Hemp: Aligning The Stars with Earth's Ancient Herb

-The Astrological Guide to Hemp: Stars, Signs, and Sacred Leaves

-Green Growth: Innovative Marketing Strategies for your Hemp Products and Dispensary

-Cosmic Cannabis

-Astrological Munchies

-Henry The Hemp

-Zodiacal Roots: The Astrological Soul Of Hemp

- Green Constellations: Intersection of Hemp and Zodiac

-Hemp in The Houses: An astrological Adventure Through The Cannabis Galaxy

-Galactic Ganja Guide

Heavenly Hemp

Zodiac Leaves

Doctor Who Astrology

Cannastrology

Stellar Satvias and Cosmic Indicas

Celestial Cannabis: A Zodiac Journey

AstroHerbology: The Sky and The Soil: Volume 1

AstroHerbology:Celestial Cannabis:Volume 2

Cosmic Cannabis Cultivation

The Starry Guide to Herbal Harmony: Volume 1

The Starry Guide to Herbal Harmony: Cannabis Universe: Volume 2

Yugioh Astrology: Astrological Guide to Deck, Duels and more

Nightmare Mansion: Echoes of The Abyss

Nightmare Mansion 2: Legacy of Shadows

Nightmare Mansion 3: Shadows of the Forgotten

Nightmare Mansion 4: Echoes of the Damned

The Life and Banishment of Apophis: Book 2

Nightmare Mansion: Halls of Despair

Healing with Herb: Cannabis and Hydrocephalus

Planetary Pot: Aligning with Astrological Herbs: Volume 1

Fast Track to Freedom: 30 Days to Financial Independence Using AI, Assets, and Agile Hustles

Cosmic Hemp Pathways

How to Become Financially Free in 30 Days: 10,000 Paths to Prosperity

Zodiacal Herbage: Astrological Insights: Volume 1

Nightmare Mansion: Whispers in the Walls

The Daleks Invade Atlantis

Henry the hemp and Hydrocephalus

10X The Kidney Friendly Diet

Cannabis Universe: Adult coloring book

Hemp Astrology: The Healing Power of the Stars

Zodiacal Herbage: Astrological Insights: Cannabis Universe: Volume 2

Planetary Pot: Aligning with Astrological Herbs: Cannabis Universes: Volume 2

Doctor Who: Convergence Protocol – The Replicator War

Nightmare Mansion: Curse of the Blood Moon

The Celestial Stoner: A Guide to the Zodiac

Cosmic Pleasures: Sex Toy Astrology for Every Sign

Hydrocephalus Astrology: Navigating the Stars and Healing Waters

Lapis and the Mischievous Chocolate Bar

Celestial Positions: Sexual Astrology for Every Sign

Apophis's Shadow Work Journal: **:** A Journey of Self-Discovery and Healing

Kinky Cosmos: Sexual Kink Astrology for Every Sign

Digital Cosmos: The Astrological Digimon Compendium

Stellar Seeds: The Cosmic Guide to Growing with Astrology

Apophis's Daily Gratitude Journal

Cat Astrology: Feline Mysteries of the Cosmos

The Cosmic Kama Sutra: An Astrological Guide to Sexual Positions

Unleash Your Potential: A Guided Journal Powered by AI Insights

Whispers of the Enchanted Grove

Cosmic Pleasures: An Astrological Guide to Sexual Kinks

369, 12 Manifestation Journal

Whisper of the nocturne journal(blank journal for writing or drawing)

The Boogey Book

Locked In Reflection: A Chastity Journey Through Locktober

Generating Wealth Quickly:How to Generate $100,000 in 24 Hours

Star Magic: Harness the Power of the Universe

The Flatulence Chronicles: A Fart Journal for Self-Discovery

The Doctor and The Death Moth

Seize the Day: A Personal Seizure Tracking Journal

The Ultimate Boogeyman Safari: A Journey into the Boogie World and Beyond

Whispers of Samhain: 1,000 Spells of Love, Luck, and Lunar Magic: Samhain Spell Book

Apophis's guides:Witch's Spellbook Crafting Guide for Halloween

Frost & Flame: The Enchanted Yule Grimoire of 1000 Winter Spells

The Ultimate Boogey Goo Guide & Spooky Activities for Halloween Fun

Harmony of the Scales: A Libra's Spellcraft for Balance and Beauty

The Enchanted Advent: 36 Days of Christmas Wonders

Nightmare Mansion: The Labyrinth of Screams

Harvest of Enchantment: 1,000 Spells of Gratitude, Love, and Fortune for Thanksgiving

The Boogey Chronicles: A Journal of Nightly Encounters and Shadowy Secrets

The 12 Days of Financial Freedom: A Step-by-Step Christmas Countdown to Transform Your Finances

Sigil of the Eternal Spiral Blank Journal

A Christmas Feast: Timeless Recipes for Every Meal

Holiday Stress-Free Solutions: A Survival Guide to Thriving During the Festive Season

Yu-Gi-Oh! Holiday Gifting Mastery: The Ultimate Guide for Fans and Newcomers Alike

Holiday Harmony: A Hydrocephalus Survival Guide for the Festive Season

Celestial Craft: The Witch's Almanac for 2025 – A Cosmic Guide to Manifestations, Moons, and Mystical Events

Doctor Who: The Toymaker's Winter Wonderland

Tulsa King Unveiled: A Thrilling Guide to Stallone's Mafia Masterpiece

Pendulum Craft: A Complete Guide to Crafting and Using Personalized Divination Tools

Nightmare Mansion: Santa's Eternal Eve

Starlight Noel: A Cosmic Journey through Christmas Mysteries

The Dark Architect: Unlocking the Blueprint of Existence

Surviving the Embrace: The Ultimate Guide to Encounters with The Hugging Molly

The Enchanted Codex: Secrets of the Craft for Witches, Wiccans, and Pagans

Harvest of Gratitude: A Complete Thanksgiving Guide

Yuletide Essentials: A Complete Guide to an Authentic and Magical Christmas

Celestial Smokes: A Cosmic Guide to Cigars and Astrology

Living in Balance: A Comprehensive Survival Guide to Thriving with Diabetes Insipidus

Cosmic Symbiosis: The Venom Zodiac Chronicles

The Cursed Paw of Ambition

Cosmic Symbiosis: The Astrological Venom Journal

Celestial Wonders Unfold: A Stargazer's Guide to the Cosmos (2024-2029)

The Ultimate Black Friday Prepper's Guide: Mastering Shopping Strategies and Savings

Cosmic Sales: The Astrological Guide to Black Friday Shopping

Legends of the Corn Mother and Other Harvest Myths

Whispers of the Harvest: The Corn Mother's Journal

The Evergreen Spellbook

The Doctor Meets the Boogeyman

The White Witch of Rose Hall's SpellBook

The Gingerbread Golem's Shadow: A Study in Sweet Darkness

The Gingerbread Golem Codex: An Academic Exploration of Sweet Myths

The Gingerbread Golem Grimoire: Sweet Magicks and Spells for the Festive Witch

The Curse of the Gingerbread Golem

10-minute Christmas Crafts for kids

Christmas Crisis Solutions: The Ultimate Last-Minute Survival Guide

Gingerbread Golem Recipes: Holiday Treats with a Magical Twist

The Infinite Key: Unlocking Mystical Secrets of the Ages

Enchanted Yule: A Wiccan and Pagan Guide to a Magical and Memorable Season

Dinosaurs of Power: Unlocking Ancient Magick

Astro-Dinos: The Cosmic Guide to Prehistoric Wisdom

Gallifrey's Yule Logs: A Festive Doctor Who Cookbook

The Dino Grimoire: Secrets of Prehistoric Magick

The Gift They Never Knew They Needed

The Gingerbread Golem's Culinary Alchemy: Enchanting Recipes for a Sweetly Dark Feast

A Time Lord Christmas: Holiday Adventures with the Doctor

Krampusproofing Your Home: Defensive Strategies for Yule

Silent Frights: A Collection of Christmas Creepypastas to Chill Your Bones

Santa Raptor's Jolly Carnage: A Dino-Claus Christmas Tale

Prehistoric Palettes: A Dino Wicca Coloring Journey
The Christmas Wishkeeper Chronicles
The Starlight Sleigh: A Holiday Journey
Elf Secrets: The True Magic of the North Pole
Candy Cane Conjurations
Cooking with Kids: Recipes Under 20 Minutes
Doctor Who: The TARDIS Confiscation
The Anxiety First Aid Kit: Quick Tools to Calm Your Mind
Frosty Whispers: A Winter's Tale
The Infinite Key: Unlocking the Secrets to Prosperity, Resilience, and Purpose
The Grasping Void: Why You'll Regret This Purchase
Astrology for Busy Bees: Star Signs Simplified
The Instant Focus Formula: Cut Through the Noise
The Secret Language of Colors: Unlocking the Emotional Codes
Sacred Fossil Chronicles: Blank Journal
The Christmas Cottage Miracle
Feeding Frenzy: Graboid-Inspired Recipes
Manifest in Minutes: The Quick Law of Attraction Guide
The Symbiote Chronicles: Doctor Who's Venomous Journey
Think Tiny, Grow Big: The Minimalist Mindset
The Energy Key: Unlocking Limitless Motivation
New Year, New Magic: Manifesting Your Best Year Yet
Unstoppable You: Mastering Confidence in Minutes
Infinite Energy: The Secret to Never Feeling Drained
Lightning Focus: Mastering the Art of Productivity in a Distracted World
Saturnalia Manifestation Magick: A Guide to Unlocking Abundance During the Solstice
Graboids and Garland: The Ultimate Tremors-Themed Christmas Guide
12 Nights of Holiday Magic
The Power of Pause: 60-Second Mindfulness Practices

The Quick Reset: How to Reclaim Your Life After Burnout
The Shadow Eater: A Tale of Despair and Survival
The Micro-Mastery Method: Transform Your Skills in Just Minutes a Day
Reclaiming Time: How to Live More by Doing Less
Chronovore: The Eternal Nexus
The Mind Reset: Unlocking Your Inner Peace in a Chaotic World
Confidence Code: Building Unshakable Self-Belief
Baby the Vampire Terrier
Baby the Vampire Terrier's Christmas Adventure
Celestial Streams: The Content Creator's Astrology Manual
The Wealth Whisperer: Unlocking Abundance with Everyday Actions
The Energy Equation: Maximize Your Output Without Burning Out
The Happiness Algorithm: Science-Backed Steps to Joyful Living
Stress-Free Success: Achieving Goals Without Anxiety
Mindful Wealth: The New Blueprint for Financial Freedom
The Festive Flavors of New Year: A Culinary Celebration
The Master's Gambit: Keys of Eternal Power
Shadowed Secrets: Groundhog Day Mysteries
Beneath the Burrow: Lessons from the Groundhog
Spring's Whispers: The Groundhog's Prediction
The Limitless Mindset: Unlock Your Untapped Potential
The Focus Funnel: How to Cut Through Chaos and Get Results
Bold Moves: Building Courage to Live on Your Terms
The Daily Shift: Simple Practices for Lasting Transformation
The Quarter-Life Reset: Thriving in Your 20s and 30s
The Art of Shadowplay: Building Your Own Personal Myth
The Eternal Loop: Finding Purpose in Repetition
Burrowing Wisdom: Life Lessons from the Groundhog
Shadow Work: A Groundhog Day Perspective
Love in Bloom: 5-Minute Romantic Gestures

The Shadowspell Codex: Secrets of Forbidden Magick
The Burnout Cure: Finding Balance in a Busy World
The Groundhog Prophecy: Unlocking Seasonal Secrets
Nog Tales: The Spirited History of Eggnog
Six More Weeks: Embracing Seasonal Transitions
The Lumivian Chronicles: Fragments of the Fifth Dimension
Money on Your Mind: A Beginner's Guide to Wealth
The Focus Fix: Breaking Through Distraction
January's Spirit Keepers: Mystical Protectors of the Cold
Creativity Unchained: Unlocking Your Wildest Ideas in 2025
Manifestation Mastery: 365 Days to Rewrite Your Reality
The Groundhog's Mirror: Reflecting on Change
The Weeping Angels' Christmas Curse
Burrowed in Time: A Groundhog Day Journey
Heartbeats: Poems to Share with Your Valentine
Dino Wicca: The Sacred Grimoire of Prehistoric Magick
Courage of the Pride: Finding Your Inner Roar
The Lion's Leap: Bold Moves for Big Results
Healthy Hustle: Achieving Without Overworking
Practical Manifesting: Turning Dreams into Reality in 2025
Jurassic Pharaohs: Unlocking the Magick of Ancient Egypt and Dino Wicca
The Happiness Equation: Small Changes for Big Joy
The Confidence Compass: Finding Your Inner Strength
Whispers in the Hollow: Tales of the Forgotten Beasts
Echoes from the Hollow: The Return of Forgotten Beasts
The Hollow Ascendant: The Rise of the Forgotten Beasts
The Relationship Reset: Building Better Connections
Mastering the Morning: How to Win the Day Before 8 AM
The Shadow's Dance: Groundhog Day Symbolism
Cupid's Kitchen: Quick Valentine's Day Recipes
Valentine's Day on a Budget: Love Without Breaking the Bank
Astrocraft: Aligning the Stars in the World of Minecraft

Forecasting Life: Groundhog Day Reflections

Bleeding Hearts: Twisted Tales of Valentine's Terror

Herbal Smoke Revolution: The Ultimate Guide to Nature's Cigarette Alternative

Winter's Wrath: The Complete Survival Blueprint for Extreme Freezes.

The Groundhog's Shadow: A Tale of Seasons

Burrowed Insights: Wisdom from the Groundhog

Sensual Strings: The Art of Erotic Bondage

Whispered Flames: Unlocking the Power of Fire Play

Forgotten Shadows: A Guide to Cryptids Lost to Time

Six Weeks of Secrets: Groundhog Day's Hidden Messages

Shadows and Cycles: Groundhog Day Reflections

The Art of Love Letters: Crafting the Perfect Message

Romantic Getaways at Home: Turning Your Space into Paradise

Purrfect Brews: A Cat Lover's Guide to Coffee and Companionship

The Groundhog's Wisdom: Timeless Lessons for Modern Life

The Shadow Oracle: Groundhog Day as a Predictor

Emerging from the Burrow: A Journey of Renewal

The Language of Love: Learning Your Partner's Love Style

Authorpreneur: The Ultimate Blueprint for Writing, Publishing, and Thriving as an Author

Weathering the Seasons: Groundhog Day Perspectives

Valentine's Day Magic: A Guide to Romantic Rituals

The Shadow Chronicles: Stories of Groundhog Day

Love and Laughter: Fun Games for Valentine's Day

AstroRealty: Unlocking the Stars for Property Success

The Groundhog's Path: A Guide to Seasonal Balance

Groundhog Day Diaries: Reflections in the Shadow

The Groundhog's Light: Illuminating the Path Ahead

Valentine's Traditions from Around the World

AI Wealth Revolution: Unlocking the Trillionaire Mindset
Love Rekindled: Reigniting Passion in Relationships
Single and Thriving: Self-Love on Valentine's Day
Emerald Legends: Mystical Tales of Ireland
Green Alchemy: Harnessing Nature's Magic
The Hearts of Horror: A Valentine's Day Nightmare
The Leprechaun's Guide to Wealth and Wisdom
Dancing with the Sidhe: Celebrating the Otherworld
Shamrocks and Shadows: Mysteries of the Green Isle
Emerald Energy: Harnessing Luck and Growth
The Gingerbread Golem's Valentine: A Sweetheart's Guide to Love and Enchantment
The Celtic Knot: Weaving Life and Destiny
Green Fire: Elemental Magic for St. Patrick's Day
Clover Chronicles: Finding Your Inner Luck
Ireland's Mystical Creatures: A Field Guide
Gingerbread Golem's Love Almanac
Prowl and Thrive: The Lion's Guide to Success
Love Alchemy: Transforming Your Life Through Heart Energy
WORLD DOMINATION: Woman's Rule 3:The New Life
The Midnight Rose: A Guide to Lunar Love Spells
The Forbidden Letters: Writing Your Own Love Prophecy
Luck and Lore: St. Patrick's Day for Modern Mystics
The Green Path: A Pagan Celebration of Renewal
The Dark Architect's Guide to Reprogramming Reality
Prankster's Paradise: A Guide to Harmless Hijinks
Manifest Your Reality: The Law of Attraction Simplified
The TARDIS Owner's Manual: Understanding the Doctor's Ship: *A complete guide to the TARDIS, its technology, secrets, and mysteries*
Starlit Romance: Astrology Secrets for Finding True Love

The Time Lord's Atlas: A Complete Guide to the Whoniverse: *A breakdown of the locations, planets, and dimensions explored in Doctor Who*

Sweetheart Shadows: The Dark Side of Love and Attraction

February Fire: Reigniting Passion in Every Area of Life

The Self-Love Toolkit: 5 Ways to Embrace Who You Are

February Sparks: Ignite Your Dreams in 28 Days

March to Success: A 31-Day Action Blueprint

Ancient Paths: The 13 Sacred Principles of Dino Wicca

Echoes of Tomorrow: Navigating the AI Revolution

The Wellness Blueprint: Balancing Mind, Body, and Soul

Green Horizons: Sustainable Living for a Better Tomorrow

The AI Wealth Code: How to Make Millions with Automation

AI-Powered Creativity: Writing, Art, and Music for Profit

Extinction Rites: Rebirthing Your Soul Through Prehistoric Magick

Sacred Serpents tarot

Celestial Enchantment blank journal

Star Strains

Culinary Journeys: Exploring Global Flavors at Home

The Hollowvale Curse

The Hollowvale Harvest

The Egg of Transformation: Awakening Your Inner Power

Blooming Into Power: A Wiccan Guide to Spring Awakening

The Nightmare Nexus: The Third Doctor's Perilous Haunting

Digital Detox: Reclaiming Your Life in a Connected World

Ostara's Path: Walking the Spiral of Renewal

The Sacred Hare

Financial Freedom: Building Wealth in the Modern Age

Spring's Cauldron: Stirring the Waters of Change

The Hollowvale Pact

Quantum Consciousness: The Science of Reality Shifting

The Hollowvale Hunger

The Sacred Waters Within: A Witch's Guide to Hydrocephalus Magick

The Raven's Nest: Building a Life of Unshakable Stability

AI and the Human Mind: The Future of Intelligence

The Hollowvale Reckoning

Timeless Love: Building and Maintaining Lasting Relationships

The Raven's Roar: Unlocking Unstoppable Confidence

Raven Sight: Awakening Intuition and Inner Wisdom

The Butterfly Effect: Small Changes, Big Transformations

Taming the Boogeyman: How to Conquer Your Inner Fears

The Magick of Green: Awakening Earth's Energy in You

The Entrepreneurial Mindset: Secrets to Business Success

The Hollowvale End

The Shadow Luck Ritual: Reclaiming Power from Your Dark Side

Spring Magick for Beginners: A Simple Guide to Seasonal Energy Work

Doctor Who: The Hollowvale Conundrum

The March of Miracles: Unlocking Synchronicities in Spring

Unveiling the Cosmos: A Guide to Stargazing and Space Exploration

The Ultimate Guide to Surviving an Economic Collapse

The AI Gold Rush: How to Profit from the AI Revolution

Bastet's Shadow: The Hidden Power of Feline Magick

The Bastet Codex: Unlocking the Goddess's Magickal Secrets

Purring Spells: Harnessing Bastet's Healing Frequencies

Bastet's Nine Lives: Rebirth, Transformation, and Immortality Spells

Primal Currents: Hydrocephalus Magick in the Path of Dino Wicca

The Digital Gold Rush: Mastering E-Commerce and Online Sales

Future Shock: Adapting to the Next Decade of Change

The Quantum Mindset: Think Like a Billionaire

Sacred Motherhood: Awakening the Divine Feminine Within

The Mother's Spellbook: Enchantments for Love, Protection, and Prosperity

The Witch's Guide to Parenting: Raising Empowered and Intuitive Children

The Magick of Motherhood: Reclaiming Your Power Through Rituals

The Pagan Path to Self-Love: A Goddess's Guide to Worth and Confidence

Wild Woman Magick: Unleashing Your Primal Power

The Money Magnet Blueprint: Unlocking Unlimited Wealth

Biohacking 101: Unlock Your Body's Full Potential

The Wild Father: A Pagan Guide to Strength and Wisdom

The Sacred Masculine: Unlocking Your Inner Power

The Druid's Compass

The Warrior's Mindset

The Father's Fire

Odin's Path

Ancestral Bonds

The House That Whispers

The Magician's Code

The Wild Hunt

The Green Man's Path

The Altar of Success

The Shadow and the Sword

The High Priestess's Guide to Energy Healing

The Lunar Mother

The Sacred Self-Care Grimoire

The Womb Wisdom Codex

The Wheel of the Mother

The Witch's Guide to Manifestation

The Q2 Reset
The Ultimate Guide to AI-Powered Passive Income
Escape the 9-5
AI Feline Fortunes
The Tear-Stained Grimoire
Razorblade Runes
Cemetery Sirens
The Midnight Wristwatch
The Town That Forgets
AI Horror & Creepypasta
The Hollow Frequency
The Breach Echo
The Quiet Between Worlds
The Sigil of Tharan-Khul
Summon the Vault of Y'ha'ten
The Becoming Codex
The Profit of Az'ra-nar
The Drowned Logos
Echoes of the Eldritch Will
The Deep Ledger
Necronomicon of Networth
Covenant of the Wealthwyrm
The Whisperer's Manifesto
The Rites of Azh-K'luth
The Ark of the Crawling Coin
The Tithe of Shadows
Inkheart Abyss
The Timewinds of Y'ha-nthlei
The Spiral Labyrinth of Azag-Nirrh
The Gallifreyan Heresy of the Black Pharaoh
The Psalms of Nyog-Sotha
Black Rain Alchemy
The Infinite Maw

The Entropic Blueprint
The Oracle of Sh'guul
The Book of Breach
The Drowned Saint's Testament
Dreamcraft of the Sleeper God
The Silence Market
Cthonomics: The Dark Wealth Algorithm
Invocation of the Ten-Eyed King
Wealthbound to the Wyrm Below
Become the Unnameable
Codex of the Sovereign Flame
Rituals of Relentless Becoming
The Shadow Ascends
The Eyes Beneath You
The Will That Wakes Worlds
Silence Is a Weapon
The Mirror That Screams
The Whisper Between Moments
The Mind That Devours Fear
The Myth of the Finished Self
The Architect of Your Madness
The Voice You've Buried
The Discipline of Madness
Stormborn: Awakening Your Inner Tempest
The Mind That Ate Time
Unbind Your Becoming
The Pact You Owe Yourself
The Devourer's Diet
The Acid That Carves the Path
The Tower You Must Burn
The Breath Between Worlds
Speak Like the Deep
The Labyrinth Within

The Spine of the Sea God
Rejection Is a Portal
The Crown You Refused
The Scar Is the Spell
The Lightless Flame
The Habit of Becoming Horrific
ChickenJockey Chaos
The Gatekeeper Within
You Are Not Your Name
The Compass of the Mad
The Archive of Unsent Letters
What the Mirror Can't Show You
The Knife You Needed
Worship Nothing, Become Everything
The Other Voice
The Body the World Forgot
The Vein of the Void
The Black Bone Codex
The Puzzle of the Hidden Self (Millennium Puzzle)
The Eye That Sees the Lie *(Millennium Eye)*
The Ring of Return (Millennium Ring)
The Rod of Relentless Will ***(Millennium Rod)***
The Tally of the Soul (Millennium Tauk/Necklace)
The Key to the Locked Timeline (Millennium Key)
The Scale of Sacred Decisions (Millennium Scales)
Inferno Bites: The UnOfficial Minecraft Lava Cookbook
Rot in the Attic
Prana: The Hidden Force of Your Infinite Self
The Shadow Realm Within: Transforming Darkness Into Destiny
The Borderland Collapse
Claws of Protection: Bastet's Defensive Magick
Mr. Ring-a-Ding's Madness

Yugioh Astrology: Celestial Deckcraft and Duel Destiny (2026–2027 Edition)

The Seal You Signed: Unlocking the Power You Once Feared

The Puzzle of Infinite Minds: Unlocking the Mentalism Hidden Within

The Eye That Mirrors the All: Secrets of Inner Reflection

Doctor Who: The Toymaker's Broadcast

The Rod of Eternal Flow: Commanding the Currents of Vibration

Golden Eyes of Bastet: Enhancing Psychic Vision

The Key of Dual Forces: Balance Within the Polarity

The Scales of Living Rhythm: Timing the Dance of Life

The Necklace of Hidden Cause: Weaving the Webs of Fate

The Ring of Secret Masters: Rising Through the All Within All

Daggers of the Dying Deep

Bastet's Wealth and Fortune Magick: Prosperity Rituals of the Goddess

The Tide that Speaks

The Scrolls of Petosiris: 13 Rituals from the Feathered Eye

Petosiris and the Living Plague of Osirion

Feline Fire: Bastet's Passion and Love Magick

The Star Altar of Petosiris

Bastet's Whiskers: Supernatural Sensory Magick

The Bastet Grimoire

Feeding the Shadows

The Mouthless Prayer

The Spiral Wound

Becoming the Ibis: Lessons from Petosiris's Mind

The Crimson Coven: Cola Magick for Sweet Dominion

Sacred Cat's Paw

The Soda Zodiac: A Flavor for Every Sign

Covenant of the Crawling Flame

The Ink of Ish'Zur
Frothroot: The Thirst That Ate the World
The Golden Glyphs of Prosperity
The Etherbind Codex
Echoes of the Resistance: Reclaiming the You That Survived
Harnessed Minds: Breaking Free from Mental Control
The Eyes in the Smoke
Rootwake: The Carbon Covenant
Skitter Logic: Unlearning the Fear That Built You
Doctor Who: The World That Froths
Rootwake: The Fizz That Rewrites Flesh
Rootwake: Frothfather of the World
The Holly Pact: Blood Beneath the Mistletoe
The 2nd Mass Principle: Building Unbreakable Tribes
Web of Wits: A Survival Guide to Encounters with Anasi the Spider (Aunt Nancy)
The Hexbreaking Handbook: Effective Spells to Remove Curses
Pop Alchemy: Transform Your Life One Sip at a Time
The Mason Code: Leading in Unleadable Times
Petosiris and the Fifth Chamber of Thoth
The Ether Seed Within
The Parent of Tomorrow
Petosiris's Pyramid of Perpetual Wealth
Unlearn the World
Grimoire of the Hollow Tongue
Zodiac Weeds: Finding Your Strain Through the Stars
Aquarius Rises in the Bank
The Sugar God's Smile
The Skinclock Reversal: Biohacking the Face of Time
Debtburn: How to Obliterate What You Owe Forever
The Ice Cream Oracle: What Your Cone Says About Your Future

Silence Is Sovereignty: The Power of Being Unreadable
The Wind That Whispers Through Stone
Path of the Four Directions
Doctor Who: The Maestro's Symphony of Endings
Oxygen Grail: Breathing to Undo the Clock
Zodiacal Collapse: When Stars Devour Time
Teachings from the Red Sand Silence
Doctor Who: Omega – The Broken Equation
Memory Wipe Your Past: Start Over Like a MiB
Mitochondria Prime: Ignite the Core of Youth
A Nest of Roaches
Grub from the Galaxy: MiB Recipes You'll Never Forget
Whiskers of Power: Bastet's Guide to Inner Sovereignty
The Gift Must Cost Them: Negotiation Through Unequal Exchange
The Worm Guys' Wealth Code: Hustle Like an Alien
Bug Out: The Edgar Method for Ruthless Goal Setting
Weaving Life with Spiderwoman's Pattern
Doctor Who: The Rani's Renaissance
How to Get a Job (If You're a Puppygirl)
Speak Through Others: The Art of Proxy Power
T-Rex Your Trauma: Reclaim the Power of Your Primal Self
The Black Briefcase: How MiB Stay Wealthy in Silence
The Thirst Beyond Reason: Understanding Diabetes Insipidus From the Inside Out
Backwoods Witchcraft for Billionaires: The Pagan Path from Dirt Roads to Gold Roads
The Moonshine Grimoire: Fermented Spells for Abundance
The Nameless Geometry
The Wraith's Mixtape: Spellcasting with Songs of Sorrow
The Gallifreyan Gentleman: Silent Wealth, Sonic Confidence, and the Doctor's Code of Living

Sugar Water Confidence

Dino Totems: Spirit Guides from Earth's First Gods

Pumpkin Sigils & Ritual Smoke

The Hózhó Compass

The Distortus Discipline – Order from Inner Mutation

Witchcraft for the Cold-Blooded Soul

Moonlight Over the Blessingway

Water, Interrupted: When the Body Forgets How to Hold On

Deformed but Divine: Embracing Your Asymmetry

Hexes in the Henhouse: The Farm Witch's Guide to Power

The Reversed Flame: A Grimoire of Inverted Power

Salt, Cells, and Sanity: Reclaiming Balance with Diabetes Insipidus

King of the Broken: Crowning the Flawed Self

Moonlight Scars: Emo Moon Magick and the Art of Lunar Sorrow

Noose Spells: Magick of the Hanging Rope

The Goth Cathedral: Rituals of the Broken and Beautiful

The Cretaceous Codex: Dino Spirits and Fossil Magick

The Turkey Bones Ritual

Nine Lives of Manifestation: Unlocking Bastet's Reality Codes

Chaos Muscles: Building Strength from Twisted Pain

Emo Blood Magick: The Veins of Power

The 3AM Flood: Nighttime Urination, Sleep Loss, and the DI Spiral

The Silence Between the Stars

The Lemon Method: Sour Your Way to Success

Starlit Sovereign

The Rite of Twelve Gates: Walking the Gates of the Duat.

Cornbread and Conjure: Recipes for Riches and Rootwork

The Black Rose Rituals: Emo Love Spells and Obsession Magick

The Eternal Goodbye: Death Magick and Rebirth Rituals

Sinkrot: The Drain That Remembers

The Hybrid Mindset: Thinking Beyond Evolution

Bone Dry: Navigating Dehydration Before It Breaks You

Wreathcraft: Winter Sigils and Yuletide Spells

The Rite of Twelve Mouths

S'mores of the Damned: Haunted Recipes for Halloween Night

Rethink the Drink: A Beverage Survival Guide for DI Warriors

The Shadow Chord: Guitar Magick and Sonic

Malformed Yet Majestic: Leading When You Feel Wrong Inside

The Cursed Diary: Ink-Stained Spells of the Emo Soul

Anxiety Off Switch: Emergency Reset for a Fried Nervous System

The Energy Heist: How to Take Back Your Life from Drainers

Beyond the Bathroom: Rebuilding Your Social Life With DI

Coyote's Gift for Decision Makers

Ghoul-Goo: Spooky S'mores You'll Die For

Echoes in the Mirror: Scrying and Self-Destruction Magick

Thread and Thorn: Stitching Spells from Rural Cloth

The Mogwai Mind: Building Untouchable Wealth from Small Ideas

Be Your Own Guide: Trust Your Inner Compass

Hormones in Chaos: The Endocrine Puzzle of Diabetes Insipidus

ChronoCleanse: Detox Your Biological Timeline

The Limb You Hide Is the One That Saves You

Leaves, Bones, and Whisper Spells

The Dinosaur Mindset: Prehistoric Tactics for Modern Wealth

Clawing Back Control: A Bastet Method for Boundaries and Empowerment

Samhain Codes of the Forgotten

Orange Alchemy: The Autumnal Spellbook

Monster Within, Master Without

The Sigil That Sleeps

Hearthcraft: Yule Hearth Sigils and Winter Warmth Spells

Temple of the Purring Moon: Rituals from Bastet's Lineage

When the Earth Remembers Your Footsteps

Food for Mood: Eat to Heal Depression, Not Just Survive It

Witch of the Kudzu Vine: Southern Pagan Wealth Secrets

The Invisible Diagnosis: Advocating for Yourself With DI

The Coffin's Lullaby: Sleep Magick and Nightmares as Portals

Ashes of the Will: Rituals for Erasing the Self

The Fracture Rite: Shattering the Magickal Core

Funeral Candles: The Art of Emo Flame Magick

The Black Grimoire: A Blank Ritual for Writing in Absence

Phantom Thirst: A Halloween Survival Guide for Diabetes Insipidus

The Hollow Crown: Emo Royalty and Magick of the Outcast King

Sandpainting for the Soul

Falling Into Balance: Using the Extra Hour to Recalibrate Life

100 Southern Superstitions That Still Work

The DI Child: A Parent's Guide to Raising Hydrated, Happy Kids

The Jungle of Shame: Escaping the Hidden Lab of Doubt

The Witch's Toast: S'mores Spells and Creepy Confections

The Hoodoo Pantry: Spells from the Mason Jar

The Immortal Fortune: Secret Wealth Lessons from Captain Jack Harkness

The Specter's Embrace: Magick for Channeling Ghostly Lovers

Grateful Waters: A Thanksgiving Survival Guide for Diabetes Insipidus

The Seizure Gospel

Harvestbind: Autumn Sigils and Samhain Spells

Doctor Who: The Algorithmic Awakening

Silent Nights, Steady Waters: A Christmas Survival Guide for Diabetes Insipidus

The Extra Hour Effect: How One Hour Can Transform Everything

Blade Between the Breaths

Running with the Mountain Shadows

Echoes of the Failed Experiment – Becoming a Living Legacy

Swamp Witches & River Ghosts: Real Southern Hauntings

Cornbread Prophecies: Magical Recipes from a Southern Table

Doctor Who: The Signal in the Star

Bloomcraft: Spring Sigils and Equinox Enchantments

Vanisher: How to Disappear from the Internet Without Losing Your Life

The Ultimate Christmas Cookie Cookbook

The Unbreakable Parent: How to Mentally Survive Raising Kids in a Broken World

Time Debt: How to Reclaim the Hours You Didn't Know You Lost

One Month, One Million: Unconventional Cash Creation Tactics

Doctor Who: The Cyber Conversion Protocol

Black Friday Frenzy: The Art of Finding Hidden Online Deals

The Grimoire Buried Under the Apple Tree

Digital Couponing Masterclass: Your Step-by-Step Guide to Black Friday Savings

The Fire Inside the Flint

Shadows on the Ceiling: The Emo Guide to Astral Magick

The Bone-Eaters Beneath Us

Black Friday Bundle Blueprint: Creating Irresistible Product Packages for Maximum Sales

Thirteen Nights of Unbinding

Doctor Who: Engines of Influence

Pumpkin Spice Alchemy: Recipes of Fire and Frost

When Raptor Met Rexy: Prehistoric Lessons in Wild Romance

Oblivion's Candle: Burn the Path Behind You

Campfire Curses and Chocolate: A Halloween S'mores Grimoire

The Wallet That Wasn't Mine: Breaking Free from Inherited Scarcity

The Cola Zodiac: What Your Fizz Says About Your Fate

Frostfire Fortune: Unlocking Winter's Hidden Prosperity

Signal Jamming: Detox Your Brain from Info Overload

The Dust of the Forgotten Rite

The Golden Cat Sigils: Drawing Power in Bastet's Name

Mud Magick: The Prosperity of Getting Dirty

Savory Spicefall: Beyond the Pumpkin Pie

Pumpkin Spice Apothecary Kitchen

The Pumpkin Spice Economy: Turning Trends into Billions

The Ember Veil: 13 Nights of Fire Magick

Financial Freeze: When Earning Triggers Panic

The Gingerbread Alchemist: Sweet Recipes with a Twist

Biosynth Power: Programming Yourself from Scratch

Echoes from the Talking Circle

Truffle Alchemy: Fungus of Fortune

Spores of Power: The Truffle Witch's Handbook

Doctor Who: The Tower That Speaks

The Mycelium Veil: Truffle Magick Unbound

Broke But Ashamed: Healing the Shame Wound of Debt

The Evergreen Mind: Growth Through Winter Stillness

The Black Veil Truffle Rite

The Voice Beneath Symbols

Witchlight on the Bayou: Swamp Spells for Sovereignty

I Grew Up Poor and Now I Sabotage My Success

The Lantern of Hollow Souls

Shutdown Survival: A Citizen's Guide to Thriving When Government Stops

When Abundance Feels Like a Threat: Healing the Hidden Fears of Enough

The Scarecrow Grimoire

Owls of the October Veil

Candlewax and Curses: A Halloween Spellbook

Excavating the Inner Fossil – Transforming Fossilized Thoughtforms into Tools of Power

The Yule Witch's Spellbook: Magick for the Holiday Season

Haunted Christmas: Ghost Stories for Winter Nights

The Christmas Survival Guide: Thriving Through the Chaos

The Bone Orchard Rites

Haunted Commerce: The Ghost in the Marketplace

When Money Triggers the Inner Child

Silent Night with the Silence: A Christmas Thriller

The Lightning Crown: Living and Leading Through Seizures

TARDIS Tidings: Festive Stories from the Whoniverse

Autumn Reset: Slowing Down Without Falling Behind

The Trillion Dollar Soul: Rewriting the Currency of Reality

Truffle Eclipse Magick

Micro-Manifestations: Quick Magick That Works

5-Minute Rituals for Busy Witches

The Marshmallow Massacre: Halloween Treats with a Sinister Twist

Blood and Blackberry Thorns

Magickal Mornings: Rituals for a Blessed Christmas Day

Embers of the All-Hallows Fire

The Pumpkin Market Collapse

The Hour You Gained: Transforming Time Into Power

The Chamber Must Be Sealed: Mastering the Power of Controlled Access

The Cursed Manuscript of Petosiris

The Festive Hearth: Creating Holiday Traditions

Darkness Rising: Thriving as Nights Grow Longer

Harvesting Time: Turning the Year's End Into Your New Beginning

Petosiris and the 13th Zodiac Key

Wagewound: When Paychecks Become Identity Prisons

Walls That Watch

The Silent Feast: Rituals of Power in the Longest Night

The Distortus Legacy : Becoming a Deformed King in a Perfect World

The Hollow Masks

The Gratitude Furnace: Forging Gold from Thanks

Feast of Inner Gold: Eating for Energy and Enlightenment

Haunted Commerce: The Season of Spending Spirits

Fear Bonds: How Panic Creates Profit

Black Friday E-Commerce Playbook: Sales Tactics to Skyrocket Your Holiday Revenue

Budgeting for Black Friday: A Holiday Savings Planner

Haunting the Harvest Moon

The Warrior's Water: Emergency Preparedness for People With DI

The First Sip of the Year: A New Year's Survival Guide for Diabetes Insipidus

Doctor Who: The Thirteenth Node

The Unseen Struggle: Mental Health, Anxiety, and Chronic Thirst

The Hearth's Hidden Ledger: Counting Energies as Currency

The Gift Alchemist: Turning Any Offering Into Gold

The Papyrus of the Bound Spirit

The Magick of Leftovers: Transmutation in the Fridge

Frost and Fortune: Christmas Wealthcraft for the Modern Magus

Last-Minute Gifts: Creative Ideas on a Budget

10 Secrets to Surviving Holiday Crowds

The Witch's Dow Jones

The Witches' Graveyard Shift

Pumpkin Sigils: Carving Rites for Midnight Power

The Secret Shopper's Black Friday Guide: How to Get Early Access and VIP Deals

Fever in the Foundation

The Neuralyzer Reset: Reprogram Your Morning Routine

Lightning Lessons of the White Painted Woman

The Enchanted Snowflake

The Magic Sip: Surviving Disney Parks with Diabetes Insipidus

The One Who Draws Through You

Santa's Secrets: A Magical Holiday Planner

Silent Bells, Loud Miracles: Self-Help for the Season of Stillness

The Sugar Spell Codex: Confectionary Magick of Christmas

Autumn Hexcraft: Fallen Leaves, Fallen Barriers

Sleep Like a Fortress: Build a Life Where Insomnia Can't Survive

Nowhere Was Ever Home

Christmas Under the Stars: A Celestial Holiday Guide

Rentproof: How to Never Be Evicted Again

Workless: Escape the 9-5 Without Being Broke

The Gilded Gift: A Wealth Altar for Christmas Morning

The Black Friday Grimoire

The Hollowing: Ceremonies of Spiritual Collapse

Doctor Who: The Nameless Signal

Where the Eagle Hides His Courage

The Dwarf Tyrant's Ascent: Claiming Power in a World of Giants

The Currency of the Dead: Trading with Spectral Bankers

The Icebound Witch: Survival and Magick in the Cold

The Emergency Money Mind: Constant Crisis, Zero Calm

Thirst & Roses: A Valentine's Survival Guide for Diabetes Insipidus

Springing Into Clarity: Mastering the Energy Shift of Daylight Saving

Speed of the Nanotyrant: Agile Strategies for Life's Hunt

The 90-Day Reset: A Science-Backed Guide to Reinvent Yourself Before the New Year

The Coil of Thorns

Timegates Unleashed

Dopamine Fasting 2.0: Rewiring Your Brain in a World of Overstimulation

The Nanotyrannus Mutation: Embracing Your Differentiated Form

Unwritten January: How to Use the Blank Page of the Year to Re-Author Your Life

Feast of the Forgotten Spirits: Ancestor Magick for the Holidays

The Burnout Codex: A System for Thriving Beyond Stress

I Don't Deserve to Have Money

When the King Doesn't See You: The Shadow Predator's Guide

The Reset Ritual :A Guide to Shedding Last Year's Weight—Emotional and Physical—by Spring Cleaning Your Soul

Calendar Alchemy: Learn to Bend Time and Productivity around Your Natural Rhythms

The Mirror Contract: A One-Sentence Agreement with Yourself that Unlocks Real Change

The Nile Formula: Sacred Flow for Millionaire Minds

Forward Momentum: Productivity Rituals for the Lost Hour

Harvest Gold: Wealth Magick of Pumpkin Spice Commerce

The Magick of Christmas Lights: Illuminating Holiday Rituals

Cranberry Crown: Royal Self-Worth through Ritual Meals

Petosiris and the Worms of the Feathered Throne

The Evergreen Equation: Self-Help for Sustained Growth

The Rain Will Wash Us Away: Emo Weather Magick

Snowlight Shadows: Magick Under Frozen Stars

Doctor Who: Merger of Empires

The Light Within the Feast: Magickal Wealth of Yuletide Flame

Momentum Machines: Small Habits Designed to Snowball into Unstoppable Forward Motion

Calm Spells: Magickal Solutions for Anxiety Relief

Santa's Final List: The Naughty Never Leave

The Mystic's Guide to Banishing Worry

The Silence Dividend: Turning Quiet Mornings into Compounding Growth All Year

Charmed Stillness: Rituals to Ease the Mind

Blood Spiral Ascension

The Vanishing Heart Invocation

Crystal Calm: Harnessing Stones for Anxiety

The Nano Tyrant Code: Strength in the Small Predator

The Energy Ledger: Accounting Methods for Vitality, Not Just Money

Snowglobe Mindset: Shake Up Your Thoughts, Settle Into Peace

The Weight of the Feather: Anubis's Codes for Soul Balance

Pocket Peppermint Power: Tiny Rituals for Big Holiday Energy

Shadowkeeper of the Golden Jackal: Anubis's Path to Energetic Protection

The Tenth Doctor: The Lonely Hero (David Tennant, 2005–2010)

The Eleventh Doctor: The Madman in a Box (Matt Smith, 2010–2013)

The Twelfth Doctor: The Rebel with a Cause (Peter Capaldi, 2013–2017)

The Thirteenth Doctor: Breaking the Mold
(Jodie Whittaker, 2017–2022)

The Fourteenth Doctor: A New Beginning (David Tennant, 2022–2023)

The Fifteenth Doctor: Rewriting the Stars
(Ncuti Gatwa, 2023–2025)

Santa's Shortcut to Success: Micro Habits for a Better New Year

The Midnight Cocoa Manifesto: Comfort Rituals for Hard Nights

Why I Can't Save: Trauma Blocks to Financial Planning

Dino Brain, Mega Goals: Rewire Yourself for Savage Success.

Jurassic Profit: Unearth Your Inner Millionaire Fossil

Scales & Softness: Dating with Dino Heart

Carnotaurus Dreams.

Red Willow Thinking.

Reindeer Resilience: How to Keep Going When You're Exhausted

Candlewick Courage: Lighting Strength in Dark Seasons.

Elf-Mode Focus: Fast Attention Fixes for Busy Seasons

Futureproof Feelings: Emotional Skill-Building for Resilience No Matter What the New Year Brings

The 90-Day Rewire: Transform Your Neural Pathways Before Spring Blooms

Jolly Rich: Christmas Micro-Money Magick for Fast Prosperity.

Gingerbread Gratitude: Mini Practices for a Happier Holiday

Trauma-Spending: When Money Becomes a Drug

Goal Skeletons: Build Minimalist Frameworks for Resolutions That Last

The Snarl Strategy: Growling Back at a World That Silenced You

The Hourglass Reset: Reclaiming What the Clock Took

Yule Claw: Dino Rites of Light in the Darkness

Sacred Circles: Grounding Rituals for Anxious Souls

Clockstopper's Gut: Rebuilding the Core of Time

Winterfire Drive: Harness the Cold Season's Stillness to Ignite Deep Motivation

The 5-Minute Productivity Hack: Small Steps to Big Results

Light Ascending: A Self-Help Guide to Longer Days

Inner Economy: Trade Self-Doubt for Confidence Like a High-Value Currency

Simple Success: Decluttering Your Life for Better Results

The Resilient Mind: Thriving in Tough Times

The 2026 Playbook: Mastering the Year Ahead

The Spring Sleep Solution: Conquering Fatigue After Time Change.

The Hormonal Compass: Navigate Back to Your Youth

Golden Vision: Eating for Your Eye Color with the Power of Ghee

Lionhearted Love: Strength in Relationships

MiB Mindset: Think Like a Cosmic Agent

The Ladder of Small Wins: Climb Out of Stagnation by Stacking Micro-Victories

The Momentum Hour: Gaining More in Less Time.

The Year of You: A Self-Help Blueprint for Unapologetic Self-Ownership

The Dust That Watches You Back.

The Astral Parent

Shadow of the King: The Nanotyrannus Parable

Tiny Tidings of Triumph: Small Wins That Change Your Life
Dwarf Tyrant Rising: When You're the One They Overlook
The Bank Account Mirror: Healing How You See Yourself Through Money
Cretaceous Black
When Love Costs Too Much: Romantic Triggers and Financial Wounds
Dream-Eater's Guide to Wealth
Unzipped Reality: The Jacket That Opens Portals
The Power of No: How to Set Boundaries and Get Rich
Keeper of the Desert Veil: Anubis's Teachings on Illusion & Truth
Redacted Stargates: Stories the SGC Buried
The Clock That Dripped Time
Doctor Who: The Silent Acquisition
Hairline Manifestation: Unlocking Power at the Edge of Thought
Cash-Eater Crickets: How Insects Predict Economic Collapse
Dead Pet Whisperer: Grief Alchemy from the Other Side
The Love Algorithm Is Broken: Hack Romance Before It Hacks You
The Rite of the 8-Limbed Seal
Melt the Moon: A Fire Ritual to Reshape Emotion
Venomous Miracles: Healing Through the Poison Path
Wealth Without Water: The Post-Aquatic Rich Life
The Butterfly Betrayal: When Change Turns on You
The Quiet Upgrade: How Humans Are Secretly Rebuilding Themselves Without Asking Permission
Nobody Taught Us This: The Missing Human Manual for Money, Energy, and Self-Respect
You Were Never Broken: Why Most People Are Reacting Normally to an Unstable World

After the Noise Ends: How Humans Reset When the World Finally Goes Quiet

The Month That Tells the Truth: Why January Reveals What the Rest of the Year Hides

Tremors Party Unleashed: The Ultimate Guide to a Graboids Birthday Bash

Cold Start Human: Rebooting Motivation Without Forcing Momentum

The Year that doesn't start until they say

Love Without Performance: What Connection Looks Like When No One Is Watching

February Is a Mirror: What Love Exposes About You

How We Learned Love Wrong: Uninstalling Cultural Myths About Connection

You Are Not Too Much: Why Needing Love Is Not a Flaw

The Crooked Fence Covenant: Backwoods Boundaries and Witch Wealth

The Day That Keeps Repeating: Why Your Life Feels Stuck—and How to Shift It Gently

Nothing Changes Until Something Softens: Escaping Repetition Without Violence to Yourself

Same Life, Different Ending: How Tiny Choices Rewrite Repetition

The Loop Isn't Punishment: Why You're Being Asked to Learn, Not Suffer

Panic at the Register: Retail Anxiety and Public Shame

The Secret Formula to Becoming an Influencer in 90 Days

The New Rich: How to Retire by 35

Digital Nomad Secrets: How to Travel the World and Make Millions

Burn Your Waiting Room: Escape the Delay Spiral

Strapped for Pleasure: A Complete Guide to Pegging and Strap-On Play

Locked in Desire: A Guide to Chastity Play and Intimate Control

Burrowing into History: Groundhog Day Through the Ages

The Shadow Forecast: The Science of Groundhog Day

Choice Cascades: How One Decision in January Sets Ripples for the Whole Year

The Anti-Anxiety Blueprint: Mastering Fear and Stress for Success

The Ancestral Path of the Jackal Priest

Winterborn Titans: Giants of Ice and Stone

The Extinction Spire

The Emotion That Made Me Millions

Delete Their Voice: Become Unreachable

The Frostbound Mysteries: Mythical Beings of January's Chill

The Roar Within: Unlocking Your Potential

From Burrow to Sky: Groundhog Day Explained

The Boogey Book: Festive Ward-Off Edition

Fooled Ya! The Psychology Behind Great Pranks

April Fools' Alchemy: Transforming Everyday Items into Pranks

Anchor Habits: Root Yourself in Unshakable Routines That Endure Seasonal Change

Emerald Waters: A St. Patrick's Day Survival Guide for Diabetes Insipidus

The Groundhog's Legacy: Myths, Legends, and Facts

Six Weeks of Mystery: The Truth Behind Groundhog Day

The Upgrade Mind: Tech-Like Patches and Updates for Your Mental Operating System

Moon Blood, Star Flesh: Embracing Your Hybrid Nature

Groundhog Lore and Legend: A Complete Guide

You Are the Lie They Can't Kill

Download a Different Reality

The Quiet Advantage: Winning Without Announcing Yourself

A Year of Gratitude: Unlocking Joy

Touch Grass: A Pagan Reset for a Burned-Out Digital World

Cold Start Wealth: Building Financial Power from a Standing Still Point

Astrology Without Fate: Using Cycles Without Surrendering Control

The Future is Remote: Work Less, Earn More, Live Anywhere

Harvest of Silence

The Algorithm Knows Your Name

April Fools' Day for Introverts

Soft Power Systems: Influence That Doesn't Exhaust You

Practical Magick for Real Life: Focus, Intent, and Follow-Through

January Is a Lie: Designing Momentum Without the Calendar

Universal Flow: Managing DI in High-Energy Theme Parks

Electric Allure: Exploring Erotic Electro-Play

The Masked Embrace: Exploring Sensory Deprivation

The Ultimate April Fools' Survival Guide

Splashproof Survival: Waterparks & Wave Pools with DI

Agile Predator, Still King: Crafting Your Speed in a World That Celebrates Size

The Shadow Feast: Groundhog Day's Sinister Side

The Bug's Business Model

Edge of Bliss: Mastering the Art of Tease and Denial

Midnight Alchemy: Rituals for Transformation Between the Old Year and the New

Punxsutawney Bloodlines: A Groundhog Day Horror

The Burrower: Groundhog Day's Darkest Secrets

Buried Alive: A Groundhog Day Horror Story

Blood Moon Markets: The Witch's Guide to Wealth Magick

The Groundhog's Shadow: What It Means for the World

Seasonal Shadows: The Groundhog Day Phenomenon
The Shadow's Curse: A Groundhog Day Horror Tale
Punxsutawney Revealed: A Guide to Groundhog Day
Safari Hydration: Zoo & Wildlife Park Survival for DI
The Foolproof Prank Planner
Latex Lust: Embracing Fetish Fashion **is a sophisticated**
Whip & Whisper: The Dynamics of Impact Play
The Shadow Burrow Chronicles: Horror Beneath the Ground
Frozen Shadows: A Groundhog Day Thriller
The Groundhog's Revenge: A February Nightmare
Burrow of the Damned
Everyday Enchantment: Magickal Practices for Modern Living
Budget Bliss: The Easy Path to Financial Freedom
Six More Weeks of Terror
The Oxygen Debt
The Ice Veil: Mystical Beasts of January's Shadows
Roots That Remember
Polar Myths: Creatures of the Icy Abyss
The Marginalia Covenant
AI and the Occult: Digital Spirits, Sigils, and Cyber-Witchcraft
Roleplay Realms: Crafting Fantasies and Scenes
The Last Clean River
Lover in the Shadows: A Groundhog Day Tale
Buried Hearts: A Groundhog Day Gothic Romance
Anubis Wept for Petosiris
The Lantern Knows Your Name
Rituals of the Last Shadow
The Bell That Rings for No One
Shadows of Love and Death
The Groundhog's Bride: A Dark Valentine's Tale
Frozen Kisses: A Horror Romance for Groundhog Day
The Creative Spark: Igniting Your Passion Projects

From Cub to King: A Journey of Transformation
Six Weeks to Midnight: A Groundhog Day Romance
Tide of the Unclean
Burrow of Desire: A Groundhog Day Paranormal Romance
The Shadow Magick Almanac: Harnessing Groundhog Day Energies
AI for Emo Influencers: Growing an Online Following Without the Anxiety
AI for the Melancholy Millionaire: Making Money Without Social Interaction
Winter's Grip: A Horror Romance Beneath the Frost
Shadowed Hearts: A Love Buried in Winter's Chill
The Shadow Lover: A Groundhog Day Gothic Love Story
Beneath the Burrow: A Groundhog Day Thriller
The Punxsutawney Conspiracy
The Crimson Pact: Emo Blood Oath Magick
The Shadows of Gallifrey: A Doctor Who Horror Collection
Whispers in the Vortex: Chilling Tales from the TARDIS
AI Ghostwriting for Emo Souls: How to Make Money Writing Without Trying
The Anti-Social Emo's Guide to AI-Powered Freelancing
Emo AI Therapy: Talking to Robots When Humans Suck
Cry & Collect: AI-Powered Passive Income for Emos
The Weeping Angel Chronicles: A Collection of Terror
Dating Without the Mask
The Clockwork Menace: Horror Stories from the Future
Tender Doesn't Mean Weak
Not a Burden, Not a Bonus
Dalek Nightmares: Stories of Ultimate Extermination
The Empty Child's Curse: Tales of Horror and Fear
The TARDIS Ghost Files: Hauntings Across the Universe
Soft Armor, Open Heart
Chosen Gently

Love That Doesn't Rush You

Financial Gaslighting: When You're Made to Feel Crazy About Money.

After the Bees Went Silent

The Soil Knows Your Name

The Quantum Magick Codex: Unlocking the Hidden Laws of Reality

The Gingerbread Golem's Awakening: A Tale of Sweet Revenge

The Gingerbread Golem Chronicles: Guardians of Frost Hollow

The Power of Focus: Eliminate Distractions, Achieve Greatness

Sacred Submission: The Dynamics of D/s Relationships

The Magick of Numbers: Unlocking the Hidden Codes of the Universe

Blood and Bones: The Ancient Magick of Life and Death

Doctor Who: The Collapse Dividend

Thesis of the Unremembered

Desired as You Are

The Energy Budget of Love

Romancing Your Potential: The Love Month Growth Guide

Seen, Not Studied

Screams from the Void: Horror Stories Inspired by Doctor Who

The Silence Is Watching: A Collection of Dread

Under the Floorboards

The House of Feathers and Fangs

Emperor Bones, Hollow Crown

Goreglyphs of the Boiling Deep

The Coven That Screamed Back

The Stacks That Breathe

Love That Adapts

Nightmares on Gallifrey: Frights from the Doctor Who Universe

Apache Ways to Heal Powerfully

Belos Left No Corpses

The Algorithm Hates You (Good.)

Starve the Soul, Feed the Flame

Romance Without Apology

The Carbon Illusion

Your Nervous System is Your GPS

Where Rest Learns Your Name: Six Gentle Bedtime Stories for Minds That Work Differently

Soft Armor for Tender Nights: Six 5-Minute Bedtime Stories for Hearts That Have Been Hurt

Paws of Night, Path of Stars: Six 5-Minute Bedtime Stories Guided by Bastet and Anubis

When the Mind Needs a Lamp: Six 5-Minute Bedtime Stories for Gentle Mental Health Care

Imbolc Roar: Awakening the Dino Flame

The Titan Never Died

Witchflesh Harvest

Become the Thought They Can't Unsee

Golden Threads: The Sensuality of Body Worship

Chains of Desire: Exploring the Beauty of Restraint

Glyphs Written in Organs

Living Below the Line

Palismen Don't Scream—Until They Do

The Boiling Isles Devour the Weak

Hexside Anatomy Lab

Philip Wittebane and the First Body

Money PTSD: When Trauma Hijacks Your Finances

Brother, Bone, and Betrayal

Lipstick Like a Weapon: A Goth Girl's Guide to Emotional Dominance, Boundaries, and Quiet Intimidation

The Scar Is the Portal

www.ingramcontent.com/pod-product-compliance
Lightning Source LLC
LaVergne TN
LVHW022005200926
848481LV00007B/2243
9798295607172